(ᴄₖ out our onl`
to renew or res`
www.birming`
www.birm`

SELECTED POEMS
1956–1986

ANNE STEVENSON

Selected Poems

1956–1986

Oxford   New York

OXFORD UNIVERSITY PRESS

1987

Oxford University Press, Walton Street, Oxford OX2 6DP

Oxford New York Toronto
Delhi Bombay Calcutta Madras Karachi
Petaling Jaya Singapore Hong Kong Tokyo
Nairobi Dar es Salaam Cape Town
Melbourne Auckland

and associated companies in
Beirut Berlin Ibadan Nicosia

Oxford is a trade mark of Oxford University Press

British Library Cataloguing in Publication Data
Stevenson, Anne, 1933–
Selected poems 1965–1985.
I. Title
811'.54 PS3569.T454/
ISBN 0–19–211973–7
(not available in USA)

Library of Congress Cataloging in Publication Data
Stevenson, Anne, 1933 Jan. 3–
Selected poems, 1965–1985.
I. Title.
PR6069.T45A6 1987 821'.914 86–21723
ISBN 0–19–282062–1 (pbk.)
(available only in USA)

Set by Latimer Trend & Company Ltd.
Printed in Great Britain by
Biddles Ltd.
Guildford & King's Lynn

For Peter

This

isn't 'making' love.
This is feeding off the substance of
what was made when we were made.

This is the body unafraid
of the soul. This is Abelardian glut
in a starved school.

This is negation of adulthood's rule
that talks by rote.
This is travelling out to where

a curved adventure
splashes on planes of sunlight to become
one perfectly remembered room,

white walls, white wings of curtain, window
screened but open
wide to cricket chirr in a field where no

discovery is new.
This is the always has been. What we do
is home. And this is I and you.

Contents

From *Minute by Glass Minute* (1982)

From *The Fiction-Makers* (1985)

Winter Time (1986)

SELECTED POEMS

LIVING IN AMERICA

Living in America

'Living in America,'
the intelligent people at Harvard say,
'is the price you pay for living in New England.'

Californians think
living in America is a reward
for managing not to live anywhere else.

The rest of the country?
Could it be sagging between two poles,
tastelessly decorated, dangerously overweight?

No. Look closely.
Under cover of light and noise
both shores are hurrying towards each other.

San Francisco
is already half way to Omaha.
Boston is nervously losing its way in Detroit.

Desperately the inhabitants
hope to be saved in the middle,
pray to the mountains and deserts to keep them apart.

The Women

Women, waiting for their husbands,
Sit among dahlias all the afternoons,
While quiet processional seasons
Drift and subside at their doors like dunes,
And echoes of ocean curl from the flowered wall.

The room is a murmuring shell of nothing at all.
As the fire dies under the dahlias, shifting embers
Flake from the silence, thundering when they fall,
And wives who are faithful waken bathed in slumber;
The loud tide breaks and turns to bring them breath.

At five o'clock it flows about their death,
And then the dahlias, whirling
Suddenly to catherine wheels of surf,
Spin on their stems until the shallows sing,
And flower pools gleam like lamps on the lifeless tables.

Flung phosphorescence of dahlias tells
The women time. They wait to be,
Prepared for the moment of inevitable
Good evening when, back from the deep, from the mystery,
The tritons return and the women whirl in their sea.

The Garden of Intellect

It's too big to begin with;
There are too many windless gardens
Walled to protect eccentric vegetation
From a crude climate.
Rare shoots, reared in glass until
Old enough to reproduce themselves,
Wholly preoccupy the gardeners
Who deliberately find it difficult
To watch each other, having planted themselves
Head downwards with their glasses
In danger of falling off over their thumbs.

Some beds bear nearly a thousand petunias;
Others labour to produce one rose.
Making sense of the land, marking distinctions,
Neat paths criss-cross politely,
Shaping mauve, indigo and orange hexagons,
Composing triangles and circles
To make the terrain seem beautiful.

But to most of the inhabitants
These calculated arrangements are
Not only beautiful but necessary.
What they cultivate protects, is protected from
The man-eating weeds of the wilderness,
Roses of imaginary deserts,
Watered by mirage, embellished
By brilliant illusory foliage, more real
For having neither name nor substance.

In March

The snow melts
exposing what was
buried there all winter—
tricycles and
fire-engines and
all sizes of children
waiting in boots and
yellow mackintoshes
for the mud.

New York

This addiction.
The ones who get drunk on it easily.
The romantic, sad-hearted,
expensive inhabitants
who have to believe there is no way out,
who tear at themselves and each other
under the drumbeats while everyone
dances, or weeps,
or takes off clothes hopefully,
half sure that the quivering bedstead
can bring forth leaves,
that love, love, love
is the only green in the jungle.

Television

Hug me, mother of noise,
Find me a hiding place.
I am afraid of my voice.
I do not like my face.

Utah

Somewhere nowhere in Utah, a boy by the roadside,
gun in his hand, and the rare dumb hard tears flowing.
Beside him, the greyheaded man has let one arm slide
awkwardly over his shoulder, is talking and pointing
at whatever it is, dead, in the dust on the ground.

By the old parked Chevy, two women, talking and watching.
Their skirts flag forward. Bandannas twist with their hair.
Around them some sheep and a fence and the sagebrush burning
and burning with its blue flame. In the distance, where
the mountains are clouds, lightning, but no rain.

The Dear Ladies of Cincinnati

'Life is what you make it', my half-Italian
grandmother used to say. And remembering how
her purposely ludicrous voice pulled down the exalted
ceilings of my great aunt's castle in Cincinnati
I know that brave cliché
was a legacy from her father. His western dream
was a palace of chequered aprons. Ambition was colour
and doom as he roared through four fortunes, strewing
sheep, gold, horses and diamonds like sawdust
all over Kentucky. Before he died he squandered
his last square hundred on a silver tureen, a peacock
big as a weathervane on its lid. Then what
could his five chaste daughters do but divide up his maxims
And marry as well as they could?

6

was the use they made of their half raw beauty,
and they all found husbands who, liking their women gay,
preserved them in an air-tight empire made of soap
and mattresses. There, for years, they manufactured
their own climate, generated events to keep
everybody laughing. Outside, the luck of Republicans
fluctuated, stocks were uncertain. Sadness perplexed them, but
the aunts kept their chins up trying on hats,
called everybody 'sugar', remembered the words of hit tunes
they'd been courted to, avoided the contagion of thought
so successfully that the game kept time to the music
even as the vanishing chairs put my grandmother out
and sent my sad over-dieted uncles upstairs
trailing cigar-brown panelling into their bedrooms.

Yet the eyes in the gilded frames of their portraits have nothing
unpleasant to say. The red wax roses are dusted
but not arranged. The vellum Catullus crumbles
behind the glass doors of the bookcase, frail as the oakleaf
fifty years dead in its cloudy, undulating pages.
And the ladies, the ladies still sit on the stone verandah,
in the bamboo chairs upholstered with chintz geraniums,
with the white painted wrought-iron furniture still in bloom,
laughing and rocking and talking their father's language
while the city eats and breathes for them in the distance,
and the river grows ugly in their perpetual service.

Sierra Nevada

For Margaret Elvin

Landscape without regrets whose weakest junipers
strangle and split granite, whose hard, clean light
is utterly without restraint, whose mountains can purify
and dazzle, and every minute excite us but
never can offer us commiseration, never can tell us
anything about ourselves except that we are dispensable . . .

The rocks and water.
The glimmering rocks and the hundreds
and hundreds of blue lakes ought to be mythical,
while the great trees, as soon as they die,

7

immediately become ghosts,
stalk upright among the living with awful composure.
But even these bones that the light has taken and twisted,
with their weird gesticulations and shadows that look
as if they had been carved out of dust, even these
have nothing to do with what we have done or not done.

Now, as we climb on the high bare slopes,
the most difficult earth supports the most delicate flowers:
gilia and harebells, kalmia and larkspur, everywhere
the lupin's tight blue spires
and fine-fingered handshaped leaves.
Daintiest of all, the low mariposa, lily of the mountain,
with its honey-stained cup and no imperfect dimension.
Strangest and highest, purple and yellow mosses
drink from their own furry stems.

If we stand in the fierce but perfectly transparent wind,
we can look down over the boulders, over the drifted scree
with its tattered collar of manzanita,
over the groves of hemlock,
the tip of each tree resembling an arm
extended to a drooping forefinger,
down, down, over the whole, dry, difficult
train of the ascent, down to the lake
with its narrow, swarming edges where the little white boats
are moving their oars like waterbugs.

Nothing but the wind makes noise.
The lake, transparent to its greeny brown floor,
is everywhere else bluer than the sky.
The boats hardly seem to touch its surface. Just as
this granite is something that does not really touch us,
although we stand on it and see the colour of its flowers.
The wind is strong without knowing that it is wind.
The twisted tree that is not warning or supplicating
never considers that it is not wind.
If we were to stay here a long time,
lie here like wood on these waterless beaches,
we would forget our names, would remember that
what we first wanted had something to do with stones,
the sun, the thousand colours of water,
brilliances,   blues.

The Traveller

You'd think that in this foreign place,
More strange with every word and face,
Where taste and touch and sight demand
New habits of the eye and hand,
It would be easy to repeal
The laws by which we know and feel.

I told my head it would be so;
I left my ghosts, I planned to go
And lure from every parapet
Each older, wiser one I met.
Therefore I emptied out my skin,
Or thought I had, to let them in.

I found a town I loved at sight
(The streets danced deep into the night
And all the cottages were white.)
I found an inn, I found a room
With casements crisscrossed like a loom,
And beams and ivy and a faint
Perfume of wine mixed with the paint.

Unpacked and clean, I ordered tea
And waited for my company.
No one came. The room grew tall.
Outside the rain began to fall
While pieces of a yellow tree
Broke off and smashed like pottery.
I watched them drop, I ate, I rose,
I looked beneath my hair. I froze—
My ghosts were standing there in rows.

REVERSALS

Reversals

Clouds—plainsman's mountains—
islands—inlets—flushed archipelagos—
begin at the horizon's illusory conclusion,
build in the curved dusk
more than what is usually imaginary,
less than what is sometimes accessible.
Can you observe them without recognition?

Are there no landscapes at your blurred edges
that change continually away from what they are?
that will not lie, solid, in your clenched eye?
Or is love, in its last metamorphosis, arable,
less than what was sometimes imaginary,
more than what was usually accessible,
full furrows harvested, a completed sky.

Dreaming of Immortality in a Thatched Hut

(After the painting by Chin Ch'ang-t'ang)

Drowsing over his verses or drifting
lazily through the sutras,
he blinked in the hazy August silence
through which a blind stream bore on
and the locusts endlessly sawed, performing mistakes
and catching themselves up again like nervous musicians.

The soft rain dropped on the dust at nightfall,
dawns poured revelations over the peaks
until, as he slept, he could see it all—
the graceful ascent from the shelving eaves of the hut.
The ease of detachment. The flowing out of his sleeves.
The slow half sorrowful movement of regret
as he rose with the steadying mists about his knees,
away from the rocks and the stunted, gripping pine
and the books stacked neatly out of the way of the rain.

Sous-entendu

Don't think

that I don't know
that as you talk to me
the hand of your mind
is inconspicuously
taking off my stocking,
moving in resourceful blindness
up along my thigh.

Don't think
that I don't know
that you know
everything I say
is a garment.

Aubade

Intervention of chairs at midnight.
The wall's approach, the quirkish ambivalence
of photographs, today in daylight,
mere pieces of balance. My brown dress,
tossed, messed, upheld by the floor.
Rags of ordinary washed light
draped as to dry on the brown furniture.
And the big bed reposed, utterly white,
that ached our darkness, rocked our weight.

The Takeover

What am I to do? Where am I to go?
The house has been entirely taken over by women.
To every corner they have brought their respectable destruction.
Listen and you can hear them bustling in my lost rooms,
sorting the dust into piles, embracing the furniture,
polishing, pummelling, scurrying, complaining,
pulling up the papers like weeds.

                              Impossible to know
how not to enrage them. Their rules are exuded
inaudibly, vapours which congeal into speech
only when misunderstood. They are like music.
Every woman is an orchestra. Or an explorer,
a discoverer of uninhabitable moods. If they love me
it may be because I divest them of boredom.
I am useful as a conductor of superfluous energies.
But how through their wire-like waists and wrists
do their quick lusts slip, unresisted, into my lap?
Why do I allow them to litter my mind?

They moved in politely, not knowing who I was.
How pretty they were, flitting from mirror to mirror
in their gauze dresses. How delightful and thoughtful.
I should have known when they said they liked me
they liked tidying up messes, that they needed
rooms to have taste in, that little red pulses
beat I, I, I, under the most delicate skin.
Silence is what they're afraid of. They take precautions
always to move in a pack. Knowing also that loneliness
never attacks an argument, all the mothers
and sisters and daughters glare suspiciously
at each other over the tall generations, even when
they seem to be writing letters or playing the piano.

Not one of them forgets for a moment
I am able to escape. They make it my fault
They have locked themselves up in my house.
They hate my free tempers and private indulgences.
Only the saint or the reprobate need not let
affection affect him. If I were a good man or
a bad man, I think I could make them leave. As it is,
they have made me believe in their attentions. I don't know
what I would want to replace them if they should go.

The Mother

Of course I love them, they are my children.
That is my daughter and this my son.
And this is my life I give them to please them.
It has never been used. Keep it safe. Pass it on.

The Suburb

No time, no time,
and with so many in line to be
born or fed or made love to, there is no
excuse for staring at it, though it's spring again
and the leaves have come out looking
limp and wet like little green new born babies.

The girls have come out in their new bought dresses,
carefully, carefully. They know they're in danger.
Already there are couples crumpled under the chestnuts.
The houses crowd closer, listening to each other's radios.
Weeds have got into the window boxes. The washing hangs,
helpless. Children are lusting for ice cream.

It is my lot each May to be hot and pregnant,
a long way away from the years when I slept by myself—
the white bed by the dressing table, pious with cherry blossom,
the flatteries and punishments of photographs and mirrors.
We walked home by starlight and he touched my breasts.
'Please, please!' Then I let him anyway. Cars
droned and flashed, sucking at the cow parsley. Later
there were teas and the engagement party. The wedding
in the rain. The hotel where I slept in the bathroom.
The night when he slept on the floor.

The ache of remembering, bitter as a birth. Better
to lie still and let the babies run through me.
To let them possess me. They will spare me
spring after spring. Their hungers deliver me.
I grow fat as they devour me. I give them my sleep
and they absolve me from waking. Who can accuse me?
I am beyond blame.

After her Death

In the unbelievable days
when death was coming and going
in his only city,
his mind lived apart in the country

where the chairs and dishes were asleep
in familiar positions,
where the geometric faces on the wallpaper
waited without change of expression,
where the book he had meant to come back to
lay open on a bedside table,
oblivious to the deepening snow,
absorbed in its one story.

The Loss

Alive in the slippery moonlight
how easily you managed
to hold yourself upright
on your small heels.
You emerged from your image
on the smooth fields
as if held back from flight
by a hinge.

I used to find you
balanced on your visible ghost,
holding it down by a corner. The blind
stain crawled, fawning, about you.
Your body staked its shadow like a post.
Gone, you leave nothing behind—
not a bone to hold steady or true
your image which lives in my mind.

On Not Being Able to Look at the Moon

There may be a moon.
Look at the masklike complexion of the roof,
recognizable but relieved of familiarity.
The street, too. How weakened, unstable.
Shadows have more substance than the walls
they lean from. Thick phosphorescence
gathers in the spaces between window
and black window. Something subtle, like a moon,
has been creeping under surfaces,
giving them queer powers of illumination.

In this centreless light
my life might really have happened.
It rises, showing its wounds, longing for
abrasive penances. It touches me with a mania for
stealing moonlight and transforming it into my own pain.
I can feel myself closing like an eye.
I'm unable to look at the moon
or at anything pitted and white that is up there
painted on the sky.

Fen People

They are already old when the fen makes them,
Faces without features,
Flesh with the mud
And the slatternly weather,
Green water pulled from the weirs.

Fine rain smudges their level years,
Is food for their cabbages,
Smoke for their fires,
Veils for their eyes.
They keep to themselves behind shrouded glass.

Through their small doors no strangers pass.
Their viscid souls
Spawn a dejection
Too flat for pity.
It is not even grief that takes their voices
And leaves them glazed and lost in their houses.

In Middle England

For bungalows,
For weeded parlours,
For trained souls pinched in the bud,
The window boxes apologize.

Amid highbred
Miniature kindnesses,
The spinster gardens
Make polite, inaudible remarks.

Yes, for the
UnEnglish tourist
Who lives without tea
In a terrific country,

Who cannot,
In England, sufficiently
Diminish himself,
The gardens

Are unnecessary
As ubiquitous. The wilted
Curtains, the cold
Mercenary bathrooms,

He thinks,
Would be cheaper without them.
The blossoming carpets
And the teacups

And the shelves of
Useless, ornamental porcelain
Affect, he considers,
The price of his dinner.

He swears
And departs for Madrid.
Later, in Chicago or Dallas,
Will he ever think gently

Of the ladies
Planted in pairs in
Identical houses? Of the
Jars of lilac-coloured soap?

Of the mournful
Decanters full of perfume or
Disinfectant? Of the roses,
The desolate neatness? The despair?

16

Hertfordshire

Looking down at the village,
in the wind, in the winter,
in Hertfordshire,
they saw that the chimneys were praying,
warming the small insides of the houses
as the smoke swept into the air.

Morning

You lie in sleep
as liquid lies in the spoon
and sounds trouble a surface
which trembles without breaking.
The images flow and reverse—

       the whistler, the walker,
       the man worrying his accelerator,
       the parabola of motors
       in which the milkman moves—

just so, daily,
dissolving chromatics
of the commonplace
absorbed by the listening eye—

       just so, rarely,
       the language, the salvage,
       the poem
       not made but discovered.

TRAVELLING BEHIND
GLASS

Coming Back to Cambridge

Casual, almost unnoticeable,
it happens every time you return.
Somewhere along the flat road in
you lose to the voluptuous levels,
between signposts to unnecessary dozing villages
every ghost of yourself but Cambridge.
Somewhere—by Fen Drayton or Dry Drayton,
by the finger pointed aimlessly to Over—
you slip into a skin that lives
perpetually in Cambridge.

It knows where you are.

As you drive you watch a workman
wheel his bicycle around a stile,
hump onto the saddle and
ride off past a field of cows.
A few stop chewing to stare.
And you know where you are even before
landmarks (beautiful to the excluded)
begin to accumulate.
The stump of the library.
The lupin spire of the Catholic Church.
Four spikey blossoms on King's.
The Round Church, a mushroom in this
forest of Gothic and traffic and
roses too perfect to look alive.

The river is the same—conceited,
historic, full of the young.
The streets are the same. And around them
the same figures, the same cast with a
change of actors, move as if concentric

to a radiance without location.
The pupils of their eyes glide sideways,
apprehensive of martyrdom to which
they might not be central.
They can never be sure.
Great elations could be happening without them.

And just as the hurrying, preoccupied dons
tread the elevations of their detachment and yet
preserve an air of needing to be protected,
so, also, these wives choosing vegetables in the market,
these schoolchildren in squadrons,
these continental girl-friends and black men,
these beards, these bicycles, these
skinny boys fishing, these lovers of the pubs,
these lovers of the choirboys, these intense shrill
ladies and gaunt, fanatical burnt out old women
are all more than this . . . arrogant . . .
within the compass of wistfulness.

Nothing that really matters really exists.

But the statues are alive.
You can walk in and out of the picture.
Though the mild facades harden before and
behind you like stereographs, within them
there is much to be taken for granted.
Meals and quarrels. Passions and inequalities.
A city like any other . . . were it not for the
order at the centre and the
high, invisible bridge it is built upon
with its immense views of an intelligible human landscape
into which you never look without longing to enter;
into which you never fall without the curious struggle back.

The Victory

I thought you were my victory
though you cut me like a knife
when I brought you out of my body
into your life.

Tiny antagonist, gory,
blue as a bruise. The stains
of your cloud of glory
bled from my veins.

How can you dare, blind thing,
blank insect eyes?
You barb the air. You sting
with bladed cries.

Snail!   Scary knot of desires!
Hungry snarl!   Small son.
Why do I have to love you?
How have you won?

The Spirit is too Blunt an Instrument

The spirit is too blunt an instrument
to have made this baby.
Nothing so unskilful as human passions
could have managed the intricate
exacting particulars: the tiny
blind bones with their manipulating tendons,
the knee and the knucklebones, the resilient
fine meshings of ganglia and vertebrae
in the chain of the difficult spine.

Observe the distinct eyelashes and sharp crescent
fingernails, the shell-like complexity
of the ear with its firm involutions
concentric in miniature to the minute
ossicles. Imagine the
infinitesimal capillaries, the flawless connections
of the lungs, the invisible neural filaments
through which the completed body
already answers to the brain.

Then name any passion or sentiment
possessed of the simplest accuracy.
No. No desire or affection could have done
with practice what habit
has done perfectly, indifferently,
through the body's ignorant precision.
It is left to the vagaries of the mind to invent
love and despair and anxiety
and their pain.

The Crush

Handsome as D'Artagnan,
inaccessible as Mr Darcy,
she observes him in the bulge of her
mother's teapot ... once.
There are other views. Church.
He, robed in the choir. She
behind hats, among pews.
Her eyes grope towards him,
swerve, avoid the
impossible terror of his attention.
Weekdays she wanders near his house.
He pounds the piano.
The *Fantasiestücke* weigh within her
like a dangerous possession.

The Marriage

They will fit, she thinks,
but only if her backbone
cuts exactly into his rib cage,
and only if his knees
dock exactly under her knees
and all four
agree on a common angle.

All would be well
if only
they could face each other.

Even as it is
there are compensations
for having to meet
nose to neck
chest to scapula
groin to rump
when they sleep.

They look, at least,
as if they were going
in the same direction.

The Affair

He moves off at dawn,
away from the swollen sheets,
the room like a stage, its hooded light
extravagant with gestures and features,
its revelations already hurrying away from them
as they stand and dress.

Only a door's breadth between himself
and the widening greyness. The houses
flatten themselves a little into their limbo.
A blackbird, tentatively. The first car.
A light on, yellow, in an upstairs window.

These things as they are,
on the scaffolding just as they are,
of the night beneath them.

The Demolition

They have lived in each other so long
there is little to do there.
They have taken to patching the floor
while the roof tears.

The rot in her feeds on his woodwork.
He batters her cellar.
He camps in the ruins of her carpet.
She cries on his stairs.

Old Scholars

They have written it
all in their minds a thousand times,
so neither believes that
the wound behind his lips can be
healed by her lips, or that
he could come out of the storm,
from the leaves in October,
to find in her lap
what her eyes give him
easily and lazily. All the same,
here they are—two thumbed manuscripts—
remembering mainly the
work of it, mainly
the work of it.

Siskin

Small bird with green plumage,
yellow to green to white
on the underparts, yes, a siskin
alive on my own cedar,
winter visitor, resident in Scotland,
wholly himself.

I saw him, and you, too,
alive again,
thin but expert, seated
with your bird-glasses, bird book
and concentrated expression,
hoping for siskins in Vermont.

He pleased me for your sake—
not so much as he would have pleased you.
Unless it was you he came for
and I something you inhabited
from the second his green flame
flickered in that black tree
to the next second
when he was gone.

Generations

Know this mother by her three smiles.
One grey one drawn over her mouth by frail hooks.
One hurt smile under each eye.

Know this mother by the frames she makes.
By the silence in which she suffers each child
to scratch out the aquatints in her mind.

Know this mother by the way she says
'darling' with her teeth clenched.
By the fabulous lies she cooks.

Theme with Variations

Distractions, considerations.
There are so many.
There is money.
There are possessions.
There are the professions and inventions.
And there are the men alone,
and forever those
soft thighs thought of and thought of
in empty rooms.
For there only is one love
which is never enough.

Evasions, sophistications.
They have a use.
There is booze.
There is titivation.
There is the fox on the flesh
where the breast pushes up to the throat.
There is the flash
in the groin and the long meal's
anecdote . . .
but only the one love
which is ever real.

Ovations. O deprivations!
Such semen has crept
into blonde violins,
rich horns, shy string quartets
out of Beethoven's furious genitals,
and Schubert's
and Mozart's,
that ladies who bend to their cellos,
their velvet knees apart
know well there can only be one love
which is never Art.

CORRESPONDENCES

A
Family History in
Letters

To my mother

————◆◆◆————

GENEALOGY

*The Chandler Family**

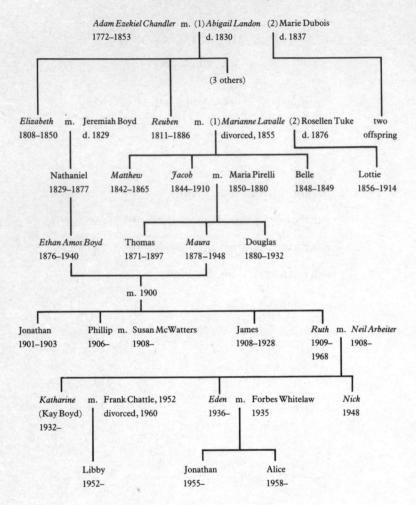

Adam Ezekiel Chandler m. (1) *Abigail Landon* (2) Marie Dubois
1772–1853   d. 1830   d. 1837

(3 others)

Elizabeth m. Jeremiah Boyd   *Reuben* m. (1) *Marianne Lavalle* (2) Rosellen Tuke   two
1808–1850   d. 1829   1811–1886   divorced, 1855   d. 1876   offspring

Nathaniel   *Matthew*   *Jacob* m. Maria Pirelli   Belle   Lottie
1829–1877   1842–1865   1844–1910   1850–1880   1848–1849   1856–1914

Ethan Amos Boyd   Thomas   *Maura*   Douglas
1876–1940   1871–1897   1878–1948   1880–1932

m. 1900

Jonathan   Phillip m. Susan McWatters   James   *Ruth* m. *Neil Arbeiter*
1901–1903   1906–   1908–   1908–1928   1909–   1908–
                                                                 1968

Katharine m. Frank Chattle, 1952   *Eden* m. Forbes Whitelaw   *Nick*
(Kay Boyd)   divorced, 1960   1936–   1935   1948
1932–

Libby   Jonathan   Alice
1952–   1955–   1958–

*The names in italic are represented by letters in this book

THE CLEARFIELD ENQUIRER

July 5, 1968

Obituary

On the 4th of July, Mrs. Neil F. Arbeiter, née Ruth Chandler Boyd, died peacefully in the Vermont State Hospital in Bennington. Mrs. Arbeiter was a descendant of the Chandler family whose history is intimately connected with the town of Clearfield. She was fifty-nine years of age.

Mrs. Arbeiter was the only daughter of the lay preacher and social reformer, Ethan Amos Boyd. She was born in Clearfield in 1909, when the Chandler House was the center of an experiment in Community and Christian Living conducted by her father. From 1926 until 1930 she attended Oberlin College in Ohio where she graduated *Phi Beta Kappa, Magna Cum Laude.* She was married in 1930 to Neil Freisingham Arbeiter, the Harvard historian, and is survived by him and her three children: Mrs. Katharine Ann Chattle, now domiciled in London, England, Mrs. Eden Whitelaw of Clearfield, and an only son, Nicholas, who is about to enter his Senior year at Dartmouth College in New Hampshire.

During the painful years preceding her death, Mrs. Arbeiter courageously persevered in those works for the public welfare which distinguished her all her life as a New Englander and a patriot. A founding member of the Halifax County League of Women Voters, she was three times elected to the State Board. She was an active supporter of Planned Parenthood, a member of the State Committee for the Preservation of Wild Life, and the author of four pamphlets in the *This is your United Nations* series.

She will be lovingly remembered for her selfless dedication to her country, to her church, to her family and friends. Funeral services will be conducted in the First Congregational Church tomorrow, July 6th, at 4.15 p.m. The family requests that no flowers be sent but that donations be made instead to the American Cancer Society.

Eden Ann Whitelaw to her sister Kay Boyd in London

MOSSY HOUSE

NOVEMBER 5, 1968   CLEARFIELD, VERMONT

Dear Kay. So . . . a summer.
    Four months since she died.
        And your decision not to return,
wise, I wonder?
        Because of course you're missed.
            Poor father!
He's in no mood for anger.
    Tries to live normally:
        office hours, meals, long walks.
Sundays, his string quartet.

You know what's become of the house.
    He asked me to clear it.
        Mother's desk, books, correspondences,
piles of old stuff, mostly letters.
    'Too busy' his excuse.
        Meaning that the dear couldn't face it,
the uselessness, pain of a return
    to a place she's still alive in.
For if she's a ghost, she's here,
        is this house.

Now every day I'm like my own ghost
    moving within hers.
        I blow off the usual mouse droppings
        (packing the stoneware).
I swat late wasps.
    I air out the stale rugs, blankets.
        Then sit up nights.
In the silence.
    The children are asleep
        upstairs in our childstained bedrooms.

Only I in her room,
    her blue wall paper.
        It ought to keep her out!
It ought to keep her dead to what it's come to!
        A stump with its root in her grave.
            An Amen to us.

30

Yes, and I'd like to save everything,
　　have it again.
　　　　Our summers for our children.
Picnicking, haying, those
　　　　purple-mouthed banquets after berry-picking,
　　　　　　dawdling days, naked in the brook;
or just the naming of places:
　　　　The Star Rock, The Bear Pits, The Druids,
　　　　　　the view from the hill.

It all seemed interminable in those days.

And now I'm over thirty,
　　looking back, looking on.
　　　　Hunched on the spindly pink sofa under the lithographs,
reading and sorting, rereading
　　dead evidences, grievances, a
　　　　yellowing litter of scraps scratched over with lives.

So I cry and cry and then
　　wish there were some way to justify
　　　　the release of it.
For it's not for her particular death,
　　　　but for what dies with her.
　　　　　　　Something that calls
for our abduction
　　out of things. Nostalgia
　　　　for expended generations.

Yet never more lovely,
　　this North-East, this November.
　　　　Maples, barren as wires, like
seas of spun wire
　　between the swell of the cloudbanks
　　　　and the black shelving continents of pine.
The hills turn silver in the sun,
　　a kind of necessary silver,
　　　　until the seasons converge there,
meeting in confusion,
　　the blown leaves and snowflakes
　　　　fountaining together.

Then night after night
　　I dream the same nightmare.

On the last warm day
    we all go down to the lake.
       We all drive down to the beach
at the edge of the lake.
    But the lake's shrunk away from its lips
       and lies small as a river,
and the beach is the lake's wrecked floor,
    wrack and litter.
          And the children,
they tear off their shoes,
    steal ahead of us, beachcombing.
We adults stalk behind,
      parents,
         two of us, loitering.

And the sky is very blue
  and the slick mud, silver, and the
    bare posts are like nails
pulled up out of their shadows.
    Oh, you'd say summer,
         but the woods are grey.
Then a jeep jolts down to the quay
    and two men get out. They
      shuffle a flat-bottomed boat
to the edge of the water,
    climb in and pull themselves, float by
      float by float along a net
lying slack on the harbor.
    We watch them reel it in,
      doubled, always, by water.

And then the children,
    who have rounded the shore,
      cluster opposite, jeering.

Their arms are full of driftwood,
    and their faces so clear
      we seem to share them with some
menace or fascination
    as the boat crawls nearer.
      Then I know they will be gone.
I never will be able to retrieve them.
    I cry out.
      Stumble forward.

Come back! Come back!
     They seem not to hear.
     And then the children are not our children,
but us.
  Not Jonathan, Libby, Alice, but
     you, me, Nicholas.

That's when I wake,
     usually as now, with the dawn
       grey and cold in the empty window.

Kay, please come home.
     Please won't you come home?
       Come help me keep her alive a little longer.

THE CLEARFIELD ENQUIRER

November 8, 1968

Clearfield's New Public Monument and Museum

An Historical Note on the Chandler Home

According to Mrs. Eden Whitelaw, a daughter of the late Mrs. Neil F. Arbeiter who died last July, the Chandler Home is to be opened to the public next summer. Professor Arbeiter has agreed to its being used as a museum and library, and Mrs. Whitelaw, who will continue to reside with her family in 'The Old Red Barn' next door, assures us that the original furniture will be preserved, and that a selection of family letters will be made available to the public.

The Chandler family was established in New England when Reverend Adam Ezekiel Chandler emigrated from Yorkshire in 1789. In 1800 he married a daughter of the Landon family in New Haven, after which he settled in what was then called 'Mossy House' in Clearfield. Until his death in 1853 he preached Hellfire and abolition from the pulpit of the First Congregational Church. He was famous throughout New England for his uncompromising Calvinism and for his devotion to the cause of Negro emancipation in the South.

During the 1830s and 40s, the Chandler home was a station in the 'underground railway' which aided escaped slaves to flee north into Canada. After the Civil War, the house passed into an era of austere elegance under the ownership of Dr. Chandler's grandson, the wealthy and pious Jacob M. Chandler of Chandler Stores, Inc., Cincinnati and Boston. The property passed to Jacob's daughter, Maura, on her marriage to the social reformer, Ethan A. Boyd in 1900. Boyd converted the house into a dormitory and retreat for city factory workers. In 1909 it became the center of an experiment in cooperative socialist living, the

34

'Eden' of English novelist Paul W. Maxwell's *A Second Eve*. In 1929 Ethan Boyd went bankrupt. He ended his days in 1940, a broken and tragic figure, in a mental institution in New York State.

Despite the Great Depression, the Cincinnati Insurance magnate, Herman Arbeiter, was able to save the Chandler estate when his son, Neil, married Ethan and Maura Boyd's only daughter, Ruth, in 1930. The house has passed on through the Arbeiters to the descendants of the original Chandlers who have generously made provisions for their home to be a community monument.

There is no doubt that the Chandler Home remains today a link with our town's great past. We hope it will stand as a monument to Yankee common sense and idealism at this time when the oldest American institutions are in jeopardy. In the teeth of subversion and doubt, let us keep one corner of our dear New England bright and unspoiled. Let us honor our traditions and the dedicated spirit of our ancestors – honest, hard-working, decent Christian Americans – for the sake of whom and whose children Ruth Arbeiter did not live and die in vain.

PART ONE

In the Hand of the Lord
1829–1929

Letters and documents selected from the Chandler Family Archives of the Chandler Memorial Library, Vermont, being a partial record of members of the family descended from Adam Ezekiel Chandler who was for more than fifty years Minister of the First Congregational Church of Clearfield in the County of Halifax.

*Condolences of a minister to his bereaved
daughter after the death of her young husband
in a shipwreck off the Yorkshire coast*

SEPTEMBER 3, 1829   CLEARFIELD, VERMONT

My wretched daughter,

I have studied your letter with exacting and impartial attention.
What shall I say?
Except that I suffer, as you, too, must suffer
increasingly from a sense of the justice of your bereavement.

What did you expect, Elizabeth,
from your childhood preferring, despite my prognostications,
the precarious apartments of the world
to the safer premises of the spirit.
Have I not heard you declare, and on more than one occasion,
that only if your earthly aspirations should be cut down
would you cast yourself upon the Mercy of God?

What your conduct has been your conscience will teach you.
What God in his Justice has performed is plain enough.

Is it possible you imagine you have claims on his Infinite
    Mercy?
Even presupposing that God has summoned you this sacrifice,
do you deem it in the interest of The Lord to secure your favor?

Is not sacrifice punishment of Sin?
Is it not through God's Will that we all do not perish
instantly? Instantaneously consumed!

Avoid, my child, those rocks on which multitudes have been
    wrecked!
Think not to gain peace with The Lord by measuring
Immutable Requirements with the petty inch rule of ability!
His requirements of you are but three:
Repentance. Faith. Love. Only these.
How often in my life has some Act of the Almighty
opened vast caverns of tempestuous night and vicissitude!
Yet never before have I felt so keenly, so intimately,
the power of His Unfathomable Choice.

Such a talent cut off!
Scholarship. Humility. Devotion to
Truth and Duty. All in a twinkling rendered useless by that
Hand of Mysterious Providence which plunges like lightning
into the heart of us, scooping, as it were,
but a single drop from the tainted well, swelling,
could we but see it, with the waters of human iniquity
the Eternal River of Heaven which flows from the Throne!

How can I give you the comfort you desire?
Turn rather to that Shepherd you have rejected.
Let him bear you to His Glorious Pastures
where in company with the Chosen of His Flock
you may content your soul with the reflection that
what is loss to you is gain immeasurable to that
dear one now with God.
                    For
fine as was his spirit upon this earth,
drawn down by the body which confined it—
what now must it be, washed white in the Blood of the Lamb,
drenched daily in that Inexhaustible Spring
which is the source of our Everlasting Joy?

My blessing upon you and upon your little one.
May you find in the Love of Jesus hope you had abandoned.
May the Light of His Countenance shine upon you and
give you peace, now and in the Life Everlasting.

                    From your loving father on earth who lives in
                    The Lord,

                    Adam Chandler

37

The Minister's wife, in confidence, to a beloved sister during a January storm

JANUARY 14, 1830   CLEARFIELD, VERMONT

My dear Eliza,

Your letter came to hand in good time.
Would answer it at length were it not
for vexations: weather like the Arctic,
violent storms, no wood cut. Dr. Chandler
gone to Boston. Youth from Harvard
in exchange here, sprawled by the one fire,
bawling for malmsey, concocting us morsels
for tomorrow's theological banquet while we
shiver on his polar side, hungry for the supper
our wet coals smoke but won't cook!

Anne's in bed. Grippe. And Elizabeth
frantic lest her Nathan, who has weak lungs,
contract it. Black Beck's in the pantry.
I can hear her, poor woman, screaming through
four closed doors. A finger. She crushed it
in the clothes mangle. Doubt she'll save it.

So, with one thing and another,
my reading flags. I average, perhaps,
a page a week. Must content myself,
I fancy, with the learning I possess, or
glean what I can from the backs of newspapers.
I've learned this: Alkalis are thought to be
metal oxides. How I rejoice in this fact.

But the children all ail, and not noiselessly.
Each day's a struggle. Scant food. Stacked drifts.
The horses, sheep, sickly, and poor Bob,
the Labrador, dead in the hayloft, forgotten
after last week's rat-catching!

Alas, I must stop.
My hand's gone numb.
The stove's gone out.
I pray you,
        keep well and God bless you.

                    From your everloving sister,

                        Abigail Chandler

NEW ENGLAND PRESBYTERIAN GAZETTE

September 6, 1830

Obituary
The Minister's Wife

On September 3rd, in the thirty-ninth year of her life in the Lord, Mrs. Abigail Landon Chandler, dearly beloved wife of our pastor and brother in Christ, Reverend Dr. Adam E. Chandler of the First Congregational Church of Clearfield in the County of Halifax, Vermont. She leaves desolate a husband and five children.

In the time of earthly sorrows let us remember that for this pious woman Death was not a termination but a transition.

In its infinite peace, her soul is even now amongst us.

A prodigal son: Reuben Chandler is stricken with guilt in New Orleans, having run away from restricting regimes at home and at Harvard College

JUNE 23, 1832   NEW ORLEANS

My dear father,
    That I write, sick,
        from a convent in New Orleans

may distress you less
    than that I write at all.
        Pray for my soul.

No.
    Satan has not tempted me with Popery.
        Likewise I turn from the Anti-Christ, Reason, with
        revulsion.

39

Yet I have been ill,
    disturbed in my mind,
        found unconscious on the road

by some pupils from this convent,
    struck down, nearly blind,
        from the power of a sun which,

to those bred in our blue Yankee climate
    is a weapon of fire
        in the hand of the Adversary.

Yet I do not attribute my state
    to the heat or to illness.
        A dream has troubled me night after

night in this place.
    A vision so vivid,
        so beyond my powers of exorcism,

that I lay it in repentance at your feet.
    I regret my past wilfulness and wickedness.
        I beg you regard me as your son.

I dream I am walking on one of these
    high southern levees,
        a baked and dusty road,

pitted with human footprints,
    scarred deeply with cart tracks,
        and also with the tracks of cattle,

and horses and sheep and other animals.
    This road I follow with my eyes, head
        lowered, afraid to look up or to the

right or left, though I feel,
    like a palpitating veil,
        the thick vegetation of the Bayou

looming from its moss;
    the fierce, silent pulse of the
        Mississippi; and the sun,

close above me,
    burning through its perishable
        membrane,

burning, enlarging,
    descending until I needs must,
        from the pressure of it,

kneel down forcibly in the dust,
    raising my hands to God for
        succor and mercy.

I look up.
    And lo, the dome of the Heavens
        is filled with the sun,

and its circle of horizon
    is lashed
        with the sun's fiery tongues.

To my left,
    an unbounded ocean
        breathes in and exhales.

To my right,
    not a jungle
        but a desert!

Then I look upon the ocean
    and see that it is made not of water
        but of human bodies, hideous and naked;

men, women and children are being
    swept up and dashed down,
        yea, again, again and again

into vast eddies of one another.
    And I see these are living beings,
        some of our country and county:

There is Mad Mistress Beaton,
    shorn of her rags, wig and spectacles,
        And poor, harmless postmaster Brown,

hollow, like a sheep's skull,
    but grey and elongated
        like a tangle of weatherbeaten driftwood.

41

Always I seem to see my sister Elizabeth,
        but when I cry out, she
                throws back black strands of turbulently

heaving hair and stares horribly through me.
        The next moment she is flung from my sight
                and where she was is now a coal black

negro, streaked with his blood,
        writhing and shaking his fists, wailing,
                even as he vanishes,

'Follow me,
        and I will make you
                fishers of men!'

I turn then, in terror,
        to my right . . . to the desert
                where it spills out in miles and miles of

nothing at all.
        And I pray, as Christ prayed,
                for salvation through rejection of Evil.

And then I'm running
        mad with unquenchable thirst,
                between boulders and craters and

dry mountains, starved of vegetation.
        And then I am falling,
                and I fall

thus to wake in the sweat of my sheets,
        weeping like a child,
                stared at by some puzzled black-coiffed

hag who, roused from her sleep and
        doubtful of my sanity, stands beside me,
                uncertain of what to do.

What I am to think, father?
        What is Our Heavenly Father if
                such dreams are of his making?

What is His Love? His Omnipotence?
        His Challenge? His Forgiveness?
                Even His Retribution?

Meaningless as the flesh of that ocean?
        As the stones in that desert of sand?
            Does God, mocking, squat in detachment

behind a great mangle of sun,
        prescribing to the saved as to the damned,
            my own Hell on earth?

My pain . . . the ache of existence?

I remain your undeserving and most unhappy son,

                Reuben Chandler

A family blunder: Elizabeth Chandler Boyd writes to her brother Reuben on the occasion of his engagement to a Southerner

SEPTEMBER 25, 1838   CLEARFIELD, VERMONT

In truth, beloved brother,
        this news of your 'heart's arrangement'
            martyrs the best affections of my own.

Engaged!
    And to a Southerner!
        And how, pray, tell father?

If only you could see him . . . all but
        nailed to *The Emancipator*,
            racked by the Judas-justice of this land!

Four of our 'midnight Quakers'
        passed amongst us in a month
            and with precious, brave Marie so near her time,

the burden, as usual,
        devolved absolutely on me!
            I suppose there must be *some* good Southerners.

Well, Nathan and I are as
        calm as can be expected.
            I had (with reference to marriage)

43

put aside all mementoes of mine.
    I had thought the hurt healed,
        the scar strong.

But now the utter carelessness
    of your happiness (and selfishness)
        breaks through my aching wound like a vengeful worm.

Lost, lost, dearest friend!
    All his tokens I cherish
        (corpses in my little gilt box),

his ring,
    his portrait,
        the fine, silken flame of his hair ...

they rise from the dead to me now
    like neglected ghosts
        and publish my blame from their shrine.

It happened one day
    as I sat (in tears) with *his* likeness,
        dear Nathaniel crept up to my knee.

'Who is this?' I asked smiling,
    (he saw I was weeping).
        'God,' he (so innocent) replied.

'My dear!' I reproved him.
    'Christ, then.'
        'No, *Papa*.'

'Yes, Papa, the same,' the child cried.
    'Is not Papa my Father,
        And Father is God,

And God changed to Jesus
    who died!'
        Just imagine my feelings!

I took him in my lap
    in a thunder-shower of kisses,
        saying 'Papa is *with* Jesus

because Jesus died *for* Papa.
    But we all will be with Papa
        when we die.'

And he cried . . . and even father—
    in a little while he joined us—
        cried, imploring us to pray!

And so we prayed
    and as we did, I felt
        a sunbeam spread about me

bearing in tender armfuls
    wondrous hope.
        And I saw my beloved husband

at rest in the bosom of Eternity,
    and my own soul, like your own,
        asleep on the Breast of the Lord.

So, now, my dear brother,
    may His light shine upon you,
        and give you His Peace and His Wisdom even now.

And may you be forgiven
    for the pain you have brought to others,

    from your loving and Christian sister,

        Elizabeth B.

A daughter's difficulties as a wife:
Mrs. Reuben Chandler to her mother in
New Orleans

SEPTEMBER 3, 1840   CINCINNATI, OHIO

Now that I've been married for almost four weeks, Mama,
    I'd better drop you and Papa dear a line.
        I guess I'm fine.

Rube's promised to take me to the Lexington
        buggy races Tuesday, if the weather cools.
                So far we've not been out much.

Just stayed here stifling in hot Cincinnati.
        Clothes almost melt me, Mama, so I've not got out
                my lovely red velvet-and-silk pelisse yet,

or that sweet little lambskin coat with the fur hood.
        The sheets look elegant!
                I adore the pink monogram on the turnover

with exactly the same pattern on the pillowcases!
        Darlings!
                How I wish you could breeze in and admire them!

And the table linen,
        and the bone china,
                and the grand silver candlesticks,

and especially those
        long-stemmed Venetian wine glasses
                with the silver rims.

My, didn't your little daughter
        play the queen the other day
                serving dinner to a whole bevy of bachelors!

To tell the truth, Mama,
        Reuben was a silly to ask them,
                just imagine me, tiny wee me,

hostess to fourteen dragons
        and famished monsters,
                doing battle with fuming pipes and flying plugs.

Poor Rube!
        He doesn't chew and hardly ever smokes.
                He must have felt out of place.

I was frantic, naturally,
        for fear of wine stains and
                tobacco juice on the table cloth,

46

so I set Agatha to dart in and dab with a towel,
    and told Sue in the kitchen, to brew up some coffee
        quick, before they began speechmaking.

But it was no use.
    They would put me up on a chair after the ices,
        and one of them—Big Tom they call him—

(runs a sizable drygoods business here)
    well, this Tom pulled off my shoe,
        tried to drink wine out of it while

I was dying of laughter,
    and Tom was laughing too, when suddenly
        I slipped, and fell on the Flemish decanter!

It broke.
    Such a terrible pity.
        And so funny at the same time.

I must admit the boys were bricks,
    carrying the tablecloth out to the kitchen,
        holding it out while I

poured hot water from a height,
    just as you always said to.
        Everything would have been all right.

The party could have gone on.
    Then Reuben had to nose in and spoil things,
        sending me to bed!

So the boys went off, kind of sheepish.

Later Reuben said I had disgraced us
    and where was I brought up anyway,
        to behave like a barmaid!

But it wasn't my fault, Mama,
    They were his friends. He invited them.
        I like to give men a good time!

I'm writing this in bed because
    my head thumps and drums every time I move
        and I'm so dog tired!

The only time I sleep is in the morning
    when Reuben has left for the office.
        Which brings up a *delicate* subject, Mama.

I've been thinking and thinking
    wondering whether I'll *ever* succeed in being
        the tender, devoted little wife you wanted me to be.

Because . . . oh, Mama,
    why didn't you tell me or warn me before I was married
        that a wife is expected to do it *every night*!

But how could we have guessed?
    Ruby came courting so cool and fine and polite,
        while beneath that gentlemanly, educated exterior . . .

well! I don't like to worry you, Mama.
    You know what men are like!
        I remember you said once the dears couldn't help it.

I try to be brave.
    But if you *did* have a chance to speak to Papa,
        mightn't you ask him to slip a word,

sort of man to man to Reuben . . .
    about how delicate I am
    and how sick I am every month,

not one of those cows
    who can be used and used?
        Someone's at the door.

I forgot,
    I asked Fanny Daniels to come up this morning
    to help fix a trim for my hat.

I'll have to hustle!
    Give all my love to dear Spooky and Cookie.
    How I miss them, the doggy darlings!

Oceans of hugs and kisses for you, too,
    and for precious Papa,

        From your suffering and loving daughter,

            Marianne

Fragments: Mrs. Reuben Chandler writes to her husband during a cholera epidemic

Note: Most of this journal, written on shipboard, seems to have been destroyed, probably by fire. What remains suggests that Mrs. Chandler journeyed to New Orleans without her husband's permission, thus becoming indirectly the cause of her baby's death.

EN ROUTE FROM NEW YORK
TO NEW ORLEANS ABOARD
AUGUST, 1849   THE 'GENERAL WAYNE'

Two weeks aboard the 'General Wayne'
is little more than a floating hospital
vomiting spells. I attribute them to
is truly ill. For two days he has
in his bunk.
Belle seems to recover. At least
fretful which indicates improvement.
struck by a nervous disorder.
I sleep very little and take no solid food.

(*page torn*)

(*Second page*)
Yesterday evening poor little Cookie died.
She was seized suddenly with spasms, poor thing,
and died in an hour. You will accuse me of
but it was truly frightful.
I have not slept for weeping.
only a dog!

(*page torn*)

(*Third page*)
arrived safely in New Orleans but
embark. We are all in quarantine
might be better, but Belle is
all day by her bedside. Doctor
plague and gives me no hope
pray for survival.

(*page torn*)

(*Fourth page*)
have not been able to put pen to
all over. Our dear little girl
among the blessed, my beautiful
authorities let no one near.

49

                    darkies. I am full of
               one who was without fault and so
               lies shrouded in my sister's
                   blame God and myself, dear
               why you have left me without support?

                                            (*page torn*)

A blunder rectified: A final word from Cincinnati businessman, Reuben Chandler, to his runaway wife

APRIL 4, 1855   CINCINNATI, OHIO

Nor do I wish to prolong this tired debate.
I will be brief therefore.
I arrived back from New York late
to find your letter.
So be it.
It was never in the book of my mind
to hold you by force
if I could not restrain you
by the bonds of wifely affection.
Consider yourself free.
On one condition.
That you send both boys to me
entrusting, by law,
their future to my direction.

Of the causes of strife between us—
your selfishness, your vanity, your whims, wife,
your insistent and querulous disobedience,
no more.
It is enough for you to live with your naked conscience
upon which must lie the death of our infant daughter
as her innocent body lies, unfulfilled, in its grave.
Farewell.
Find peace if you can with your sister,
her friends and fashions.
Frivolity is an armor of lace
against the mind's inner vengeance and poisons.

50

I shall send the boys abroad for their education
as soon as I am advised of a suitable school.
Respect my will with regard to the bills of divorce.
Direct all correspondence to my lawyer, Mr. Duval
(you have his address).
Now amen to this farce.   R.C.

A successful American advises his sons studying abroad:
Reuben Chandler to his sons in Geneva

NOVEMBER 5, 1859   CINCINNATI, OHIO

My dear sons,

I have just received Monsieur R's term report
and am much pleased.
He says you work diligently and faithfully.
Such work, my sons, prepares you for the time
when you will be men in this our own rich country
where labor is the standard of nobility,
idleness, wretchedness,
and careless indolence, a sin
against the Creator whom we worship.
For here we are judged and respected
according to the work we accomplish.

Summer has passed away
and the beautiful fall,
and now we have winter with its
bitter snows and winds.
Yet, on careful inspection do we find
that nothing is evil or ugly in God's Universe,
but all is for His good and wise purpose.

When you were young
you put to me many questions which,
when I could not answer,
made you cry.
Now you are wiser and older
and know as I
that religion to the mind
is as nourishing food to the body.

Little need, therefore, to urge
or admonish you.
Read your Bible with attention
and the Great Book of Nature with understanding
and you will find in both revealed
Our Good Deity,
His World in all its glory.
His just laws under which we live.

Business is good.
We number one hundred fifteen persons, store and factory.
All have more to do than they can accomplish.
It will be a busy, pleasant place when you return ...
to follow with humble spirits and pure hearts
the peaceful ways of commerce and just economy.
Nanna sends her love. Dear little Lottie
begs you come and admire her frocks and pets.
She is a bright spirit, and if we live,
will be a source of joy to us continually.
And now, my dear boys, trusting you to continue well
and to work honorably, I remain your affectionate father,

R.C.

Letter to a mother from a Confederate soldier: Matthew Chandler (aged 22) to Marianne Lavalle Chandler, divorced by Reuben Chandler in 1855

Directed to an address in New Orleans

FEBRUARY, 1864   A CAMP IN TENNESSEE

Beloved Mother,

You have left me too long, all alone,
in the land of the despot.
God grant that I soon may be able to set us free.
From this day forward I hate every Yank, as my Father.
From him I scorn to take quarter, as
to him I refuse my surrender.

I arrived in Tennessee, quite safe, without any hindrance,
though I shook in a fever of vengeance all the way.
I begin this day in earnest my work of murder.
With God's help I'll shed a whole river of
Union blood. Then Hell be my portion
if I don't make my sweaty horse swim in it!

Yours from your loving son,

Matthew Chandler

Note: Matthew died of wounds in a Washington hospital in 1865.
Marianne died, the rumor is of drink, in New Orleans in 1872.

Notes to a father from a young man gone West: Jacob Chandler to his father Reuben Chandler·

Note: These few pages were written, presumably to his father, by the
young Jacob M. Chandler in 1867. Although much of this letter has been
lost, there is reason to believe it was written as a sort of journal on a
voluntary expedition to Colorado, and was posted in excerpts en route
whenever possible. Jacob M. Chandler spent two years in the West
gaining experience as a surveyor, a miner and a sheep rancher before he
returned (poorer than when he set out) to take over the family clothing
business in Cincinnati.

SUMMER, 1867   COLORADO

So we struck across the mountains, travelling for two days
without sight of a human being. At dusk on the second evening,
we drew rein on the summit of one of those lofty hills which
form the spurs of the Rocky Mountains. The solitude was awful.
As far as the eye could see stretched an unbroken succession of
peaks, bare of forest—a wilderness of rocks with stunted trees at
their base, and deep ravines where no streams were running.

A gleam of light at the bottom of the gorge caught our
Indian's eye. Descending the declivity we reached a cabin rudely
built of dead wood brought down, probably, by spring rains
from the hills. We knocked at the door. It was opened by a
woman holding a child of about six months. She was scrawny
and lined, I would have guessed fifty, but she said later she was

53

thirty. She gazed at us searchingly for several minutes, and then asked us in and provided us with milk and corn-bread, a welcome meal.

The cabin was divided into two apartments, a kitchen which served also as store-room, dining room and sitting room; the other chamber was the bunk room where the family slept. Five children of all sizes tumbled out of this latter apartment and stood gawking at us from the rough-adzed doorway while we ate.

The woman said her husband was a miner. Four years before he had come with the family from the East. Pushing on in advance of the main movement of immigrants in the territory, he had discovered a rich gold placer in this gorge. While he spent his days working in it, his wife, with her own hands, turned up the soil in the nearby valley, raised all the corn and potatoes required for support of the family and made all the clothes.

We asked if she had ever been attacked by Indians. 'Only twice,' she replied. 'Once three prowlers came to the door and asked for food. My husband handed them a loaf from the window, but they lurked in the bushes all night. Another time a large war-party encamped a mile below us. A dozen surrounded the house. We thought we were lost. We could hear their bullets rattle against the rafters, and you can see the holes they made in the door. We should have all been scalped if a company of soldiers had not come up the valley that day and burned the red-skins out.

'There is no end of bears and wolves. We hear them howling all night. Last winter the wolves came and drummed on the door with their paws and whined piteously, like big dogs begging for their dinners. My husband shot ten and I six of them. After that we were troubled no more.'

When we asked her if she were not lonely, she gave a little cry, whether in laughter or anguish I could not tell. 'I'm too busy to think,' she exclaimed, 'in the daytime. I must wash and boil and bake and look after the cows who wander off in search of pasture. I must hoe the corn and potatoes and cut wood. We have no schools here, as you can see, but I have taught the oldest children how to read. Every Sunday we have family prayers. We each read a verse of the Bible (except the baby) and then the children repeat it until they know it by heart.'

54

We finished our meal and thanked her and gave pennies to the children, who took them without looking at us and then scuttled off into the pitch darkness of the bedroom. She said she would have liked to ask us to pass the night there, but she and her husband were hard pressed to find beds for their own brood. 'One day,' she confided to us, 'we shall have a fine house with two storeys and a carpet and some proper English china and I shall want for nothing. We are saving for a saw mill, and by next spring should have our own lumber business and maybe a dray-horse or two.'

After we had watered and rubbed down our horses we said good-bye. For a long time after we left I saw her standing by her unpainted door every time I looked back. She stood in the sun, frowning as though it dazzled her. I could not help hoping she would at last have her fine house and her saw mill. As we were obliged to reach Denver by the next day to pick up a mining party, we pressed on through most of the night. We camped, finally, in the shelter of a boulder, and I went to sleep praying for that strange, brave couple who had chosen to risk their lives for the sake of a little gold, a saw mill and perhaps a set of proper English china.

Maxims of a Christian businessman: From the journal of Jacob M. Chandler, Cincinnati's citizen of the year 1895

The Foundations of Belief

1. Christ demands full surrender
2. Give Sunday to the Lord
3. Alcohol is Satan's most powerful weapon
4. No man is beyond redemption

A Guide to American Home and Business Ethics

Work is next to Godliness; a man should keep books when dealing with the Deity.

The Golden Rule of the New Testament is the Golden Rule of Business.

Religion is the only investment that pays dividends in the life everlasting.

By doing good with his money a man, as it were, stamps the Image of God upon it and makes it pass current for the merchandise of heaven.

Advertising makes Business articulate. It is a language of faith between buyer and seller.

'Labor is life! 'Tis the still water faileth.
Idleness ever despaireth, bewaileth.
Keep the watch wound or the dark rust assaileth.'

Have faith. Only believe that you can lick a man and you can lick him!

No day seems long enough to those who love work.

We have no one to fear except ourselves.

To have no aim in life is next door to committing a crime.

Let a boy's first duty be to his conscience, his second to his home because there is a mother there, his third to the welfare of his country.

Everything can be determined by the three little words, 'Is it right?'

Money has feet and walks away, but right habits are abiding.

Economy, like charity, begins at home.

The path of virtue leads through the valley of sacrifice.

Body and soul must go hand in hand to reach the goal.

Smiles are roses along the way.

A worried father writes to his daughter at Oberlin College: Jacob Milton Chandler to his daughter Maura

MAY 5, 1896   CINCINNATI, OHIO

Though not altogether unsuitable, my daughter—your letters abounding in girlish merriment—allow me to suggest that accounts of such frivolous and literary pastimes as you and your fellow scholars (or should I say scholaresses?) choose to indulge could be significantly improved by some small attentions to spelling and the principles of grammar. A sterner critic, or one less fond, might find in your latest scribble (you correctly term it) intimations of carelessness unbecoming in a woman of grace and intuitive decorum.

Yet, my dear, I am willing to concede that a person of your temperament, torn from the bosom of her loving family, must (if she does not weep out her days in melancholy remembrances) stride into the rough world more than a little giddy with the ebullience of youth and the lighthearted gaiety of irresponsibility.

I do not reproach you for your laudable, if unfeminine, desire for a share of the world's knowledge. My advice is to delight while you may in the manifest abundance of God's world, provided that while you rejoice in *this* life you remain sensible, always, of that which is to come.

I am distressed, however (and make no attempt to dissemble my feelings) that you chose and deliberately chose to pass so few hours with your brothers, your mother and myself this past Easter. Your excuses (your studies, your scribblings, your acquaintances) make few amends for your sudden and inexplicable withdrawal from the family circle. Rather they augment the pain you have caused us.

Did I speak for myself alone, I could not in conscience complain. A father must provide for his own. Your debt to me is not one deserving of acknowledgement. That I have worked, yea toiled, for your health and wellbeing full seventeen years of your life has been an unbegrudged sacrifice. Yet once, in his days of poverty and misfortune (days you will not remember: you were

57

but a babe) your father vowed never to darken the familial hearth or diminish by a shade the brightness of your mother's eyes through the slightest reference to his burdens in private business. This vow he has kept! To this day, as you know, no shadow from the world has darkened the glow of my household.

Yet your mother suffers! Suffers, I believe, through the thoughtlessness of that being who should now be her greatest comfort. For it is you, my child, who have occasioned the loss of her beauty, health and good cheer which, throughout your childhood, so encouraged and nourished your own. Next time you are at home, Maura, notice her careworn face. Her hands once whiter than yours. Her fine strong shoulders, stooped with the years of childbearing. Think, my daughter, of who it was by your bedside when, swollen with fever, you lay in your tainted sheets, poisoning the air with your breath. Who was it who comforted you, embraced you, was at all times ready to cure, with the magic of a kiss, the bruised knee or cut finger of the plaintive child who ran weeping to her?

Maura! Maura! Those kisses were never gifts! Bestowed as they were with the charity of Our Lord Himself, those kisses were loans! Loans upon interest these many long years! Now it is time to repay them, graciously, selflessly, with little acts of kindness and understanding. For think, my dear, if you were ill, how that face would appear like an angel's hovering above you, its every wrinkle a wavelet of sunshine. Hers. Who will leave us one of these days! Yes, burdens, increased by your burdens, unless lifted, will break her down. Those hands that have done so much for you will lie crossed on a lifeless breast, and those lips, those neglected lips, will be closed forever.

This admonition I send in the spirit of Love. Its purpose is not to rebuke but to touch, to remind you of duties which ambition, it may be, has obscured. With it I send my blessing, in the hope ... nay, in the belief and knowledge that you will return to us a New Woman. Gentle. High hearted. Self-forgetful, with a sweet and winning interest in all the little things of the home, to shed upon us all and upon your mother in particular, the divine luster of Christian Peace which alone can illuminate and make radiant forever

The Kingdom of Home.

From your loving and affectionate Father,
J. M. Chandler

*A New Year's message to myself: From the
journal of Maura Chandler on the eve of her
marriage to Ethan Amos Boyd*

JANUARY 1, 1900

MOSSY HOUSE
CLEARFIELD, VERMONT

Without false pride.
Without true faith.
With little hope
and with no glad energy,
but still, thank God,
steeled firm in belief
that there is a right way
and a wrong
through our human loneliness,
I begin this New Year's
Day of my life in marriage.

Cold. Midnight-morning.
Candlelight out in the cold.
Oval on the near side
and the far of the
mimicking window.
My face on the far side
and the near. My life.
This room that I know,
doubled also, hung
there in the snow.

So the unknown begins as
reflections of the known.

Perhaps it was never meant
that I work as I intended.
Perhaps it was never meant
that I write, learn, elevate
myself as I intended.
My vocation. My mission.
What does Nature
ask of Woman?
Give to him that needeth.
Employ the hour that passeth.

Be resolute in submission.
Love thy husband.
Bear children.

For now it behoves me to
crush out all personal sorrow,
forsake the whole ground of
self interest, ask not,
'Do I love him?' but affirm!
'It is good! It is right!'

If I keep every moral commandment,
fulfil every physical requirement,
feed mind into heart,
proffer heart to humanity—
stands it not then to reason
a woman will be happy
in her season?

I do not believe it. How
can I believe it
when the darkness comes?
When there, out
there in the snow,
hangs a mockery, room
through which those huge,
slow ghost-flakes amble and fall!
Failure and suffering,
tedium, childbearing,
disease, deaths, days—
burying us all!

Yet without false pride,
without true faith,
with little hope
and with no glad energy,
I am, dear God, firm,
firm in belief
that there is a right way
and a wrong
through our human wilderness.
I begin, in this room,
this year of my life and marriage.
I begin, in this room,
this New Year. My life in marriage.

A vigorous letter from a salesman of the Lord: Ethan Amos Boyd to his wife Maura

Blessed One,

I think of you hundreds of miles away, and of our dear green
innocent Vermont and reconcile myself with difficulty to these
torrid streets. If it were not for Faith, for my earnest Belief that
Spirit is All and that ALL THINGS REAL proceed from it, I
think I should find Business unbearable. My love, I am alone
among the Sadducees!

It is to preserve my ideals in this Egypt that I've taken to
playing Moses and have drawn up a set of Tablets which, my
dearest wife, I am eager to share with you that you may be
better instructed in my simple ways.

Eschew	*Engage in*
Late Hours	Early Bed
	(Never After 9.00 p.m.)
Stuffy Rooms	Daily Exercise
White Bread	Brown Bread
Animal Food (Flesh and Fowl)	Raw Vegetables
Alcohol	An Occasional Pipe (for me)
Gossip	Philosophy
Novels	Mercy
Expense	Baths

I am pleased to say I have been successful in keeping to this
regime, and feel the better for having eaten nothing but
vegetable food this past week.

I have had time to make one or two public addresses; on
Sunday to the Ethical-Social League and yesterday to the
Woman's Trade Union Association. The Unions face a shortage
of money which your father, among others, could do much to
remedy were he Christian and highminded as he pretends. He is
not *positively averse* to our turning Mossy House into a worker's
retreat, but only sceptical as to our making a profit from it. I tell
him that is not of account!

Whatever his opinion I shall rise up from this city with my flock within a month. If he distrusts my means, tell him purposes like mine have for centuries fed the hungry and clothed the naked. Yea, even as a Salesman of the Lord shall I succeed.

I exist, my angel, in the invisible radiance of your trust. When I ponder on your loveliness, on the womanliness of females and on the sleeping allegory within that veils their Sphinx-like secret, I marvel that Man has deserved propagation in this wicked world.

> Until we meet I survive on your letters,
> Your devoted husband,
> Ethan Boyd

THE CLEARFIELD ENQUIRER

June 2, 1929

The State of Vermont, County of Halifax in Insolvency

Notice is hereby given that the Honorable Wm. A. Shapley, Judge of the Court of Insolvency and for the said county of Halifax has issued a warrant against the estate of ETHAN AMOS BOYD of Mossy House, Clearfield Town in the Said County, an insolvent debtor; and the payments of any debts and the delivery of any property belonging to the said insolvent debtor to him and for his use, and the transfer of any property by him, are forbidden by law.

A meeting of his creditors will be held at the Court of Insolvency in Burlington on the 10th day of June next, at 9.00 o'clock in the prenoon, for the proof of debts and the choice of an assignee or assignees.

Horace Coleman, June 2, 1929
Deputy Sheriff

A Letter to God on hotel notepaper from Ethan Amos Boyd

NOVEMBER 3, 1929

HOTEL RIVIERA
TROY, NEW YORK

Dear Lord,
I am ill, I know,
from my own earnestness.
I am stumbling-foolish.
Everything I have wished to do, to be ...
No. I have not done. Not been.

63

I have no learning or acquaintance
with learned colleges or degrees.
I have no profession or any patter
the world calls manly or
gentlemanly. I have no money.
Except as I sell Thy word
I am rot in my family . . . mine,
my daughter's center.
My home—happier without me.
My wife—silent.
For long periods, completely silent.

One baby we lost.
He was one or thereabouts.
His mother even yesterday,
after twenty years, in tears for him.
And now this turbulent, gifted,
unfinished nearlygrown son.
Unnecessarily,
the doctors agree.
(Curious, Lord, that both should be
taken unnecessarily.)

Fifty. Fifty-three.
And only these fumbling hands
with which to continue fighting.
This sick mind and bad eyesight
quivering between Thy Love and my fear.
To keep one from the strength of the other.

PART TWO

Women In Marriage
1930–1968

A London letter:
The poet, Kay Boyd, replies ambiguously
to her sister in Clearfield

NOVEMBER II, 1968   HAMPSTEAD, LONDON

Your letter arrived with its letters
   lunging at my conscience.

     Alone in wet London

with the wind trailing rain
   around these ugly brick villas,
     and the four o'clock night

arriving with my late lunch,
   I ask myself often
     why it is impossible to go home?

Why is it impossible,
   even here,
     to be peaceful and ordinary?

The ordinary offers itself up,
   can be eaten, breathed in.
     It counts on being dependable.

This is a window.
   This is an apple.
     This is a girl.

And there is a cyclamen—
   blood climbing out of the earth.
     And there is a blind of rain.

And now between the girl
    and the flower-flame on the window sill
        the window is a blur of rainwater.

I wonder how she felt, Persephone,
    when she bit for ever into the half-moon pomegranate?
        Did she miss ordinary things?

She could have lived
    without risking the real fruit.
        There were only six seeds.

She willed to eat nothing else.
    It was hunger.
        Without nourishment how could she live?

Eating, she lived on through
    winter after winter,
        the long year perfected,

the cold, waking rain
    raising a few seeds to green
        from her creative darkness.

But the mother smiled and smiled.
    She was brilliantly consumed, a sacrifice
        sufficient for each summer.

Should any daughter blame her?
    The mother made her choice.
        She said her 'no' smiling.

She burned the kissed letters.
    She spat out the aching seeds.
        She chose to live in the light.

Would you wake her again from the ground
    where at last she sleeps
        plentifully?

Two Cambridges: A Letter from Maura Chandler Boyd to her daughter Ruth Arbeiter in England

Dear Ruth,
   With the wedding six weeks behind,
     and the whole country, so it seems,

tilted sideways and ready to
   slide right off the world
     like a plate of oysters,

there you are in the one Cambridge,
   and here I am
     in the other.

As father used to say,
   'The true life of the intellect
     secretes an impregnable cocoon.'

Guess what? I've bought you an ice box.
   Also a huge bed, big enough for four.
     At a charity sale for the unemployed.

Everybody says I'm crazy,
   but suppose you two come back
     without a job or a house or

a bean to buy a beefsteak?
   Everything you own these days
     is an investment.

Now for your wonderful letter!
   To think of your getting to Cambridge
     in time for that ball!

What did they give you to eat?
   Was the food fresh? They tell me
     the English don't know how to cook vegetables.

67

I'm grateful for the snap of King's Chapel.
    It brought tears to my eyes.
        To think how poor Father would have loved it!

I meant to warn you, Ruth,
    before you left. I've heard the English
    take a light view of drink.

Greta's nephew, Fred,
    came back thoroughly *amazed*!
        He said he saw Christian women in public saloons!

But then Greta says that Fred
    came back with all sorts of notions.
        He said—since you're our poet—

there's a young man from Harvard—
    you ought to know about him. Eliott?
        Something like Lawrence Eliott.

I don't suppose it matters.
    These new-fangled writers don't go deep.
        Not like my beloved Dickens.

Now I must catch a train and hustle up to Clearfield
    before Philip and Sue, who are
        driving there all that way!

Give my best love to Neil
    and tell him to keep an eye on you.
        Who, dear, is Bloomsbury?

Don't be too impressed by those aristocrats.
    Hold up that pretty head
        and be proud you're a free American!

                        As ever,
                            your loving Mother,
                            M.B.

A Letter from an English novelist: Paul Maxwell, author of 'A Second Eve', writes to Ruth Arbeiter in Vermont

SOUTH KENSINGTON
LONDON

21 OCTOBER, 1936

Most Cherished Ruth,

Two years ago. Only two years, and the terrible chasm between that autumn afternoon in a Vermont pasture and that unknown spring or autumn morning when we will meet again grows wider and wider. So you have two daughters now! Kathy and Eden. Eden and Kathy. Two American girls.

The impact of your letter was such that I almost see you. You and your baby in that big shabby kitchen with the broken floorboards hidden under the patchwork rug, and the clay mugs marching along the high shelf over the hearth. There. I *can* see you clearly. You are holding the baby in the crook of your left arm while with your right you are pouring water from a jug into a large stoneware basin set solidly on the scrubbed table. The water is just the right temperature. You question it with an elbow to make sure. Gently, you are laying the poor naked scrap in the womb-like basin.

She howls immediately, but you are serious and firm. You rouse the soap to lather and you wash the head (the black mane you describe). Then you carefully wash limbs and belly, taking care not to wet the navel which is not yet healed after its brutal severing from the placenta.

The baby is perfectly clean and perfectly frantic. You remove her, red-faced and howling, to a salvational towel. Tenderly (but again, seriously, thoroughly) you dry the thicket of hair, miraculous hands and feet, the little runnels and pleats of the fleshier thighs. Vigorously you powder each inch. You snow sweet powder into the delicate rift of the buttocks. Finally, you pin on the nappy (you, of course, call it a diaper) and slip a fresh muslin nightdress—gently, so gently—over the baby's head, taking care not to damage the life-giving palpitation of the fontanelle.

When you sit down it is in one of those plain unpainted rocking-chairs, polished by generations of your grandmothers. You unbutton your blouse. Not Leonardo, not Raphael, not Bellini has on canvas depicted such dazzling, inflammatory white breasts. But you, of course, are unaware of their beauty. For you, they are not lilies, nor succulent apples of honey; nor are they two 'breasts dim and mysterious, with the glamorous kindness of twilight between them'. No. They are practical technical instruments for nourishing your child. The greedy thing pummels and sucks. The milk flows too swiftly. The child splutters, chokes, has to be balanced over your shoulder for a painful winding.

But now at last she has settled into a rhythm of felicitous satisfaction. She is happier, perhaps than she ever will be again in her life.

You? Are you opening a book? Yes. You take a book everywhere even now. (You keep a book, still, in your handbag when you wait for a bus or go to the dentist.) So you open what is lying on the table . . . is it *The Rainbow*? Is it my collection of War Poets?

The baby has stopped sucking. It is asleep. You hardly notice. Ruth, you are not reading at all. Instead you are staring out of the window where a simple frill of muslin frames (I remember precisely) a harvest of red and orange hollyhocks.

Dearest, I am dreary in London where everyone bores me with German politics. I'm so vehement in my campaign to get back to the States, my friends have ceased drinking with me. I bore them to distraction with encomia.

Nourish me with a long letter. *Eve* progresses slowly (tell me if what I have written here about your baby seems suitable for the novel). I return two poems of yours, unfortunately rejected, but redolent as always of

my own dear Ruth,
your Paul

Two Poems and a Rejection Slip: From the notebooks of Ruth B. Arbeiter 1936

Vermont Autumn

We have come to the end of a summer in this gold season.
    The year trembles.
I stare down these vistas of light, emblazoned with leaves,
as into the future of the past—its silence and memory.
    The empires are asleep there.
    Egypt and Europe.
They are locked in each others stone arms
    legible as geology.

Oh, pharaohs and princes buried in the dust of dead legends!
Are you resentful of Time that has stripped you of meaning?
Did you, like these leaves, burn away in gold rust into rest?
    Or did you, like trees, only counterfeit
    wanings and deaths?

Can you feel in old roots the new energy coiled in this
    continent?
Can you fructify as it reels out in wave after wave after
    wave of imperious shimmering?
    Look!
    It surrounds you with a halo, now golden,
    now pulsing and green!

The Short and the Long Days

All in the spell of the short days
We passed as it were through a mine or maze
Which was Time's interminably coiled cave.
No help nor any hope he gave,
Nor miracle of answered prayer;
Nor would he for our asking send
The slightest pin-point candle there
To light our end.

Groping along the hours, we clung
To them like ledges. Minutes hung
From our necks in leaden spheres
As, pendulum-like, they counted days as years.

Then change of sun made Time our friend.
Look how he lights with sky our ways!
How short the distance to the end
Of these long days.

The Poetry Review

The Editor regrets that he is
unable to make use of your
MSS. He is grateful for the
opportunity of considering
your work, and is sorry that
pressure of time makes it
impossible for him to write a
personal letter.

A Love Letter:
Ruth Arbeiter to Major Paul Maxwell

SEPTEMBER 3, 1945   CLEARFIELD, VERMONT

Dearest,

You must know that I think of you continually,
often entering unexpectedly
that brighter isolate planet where we two live.
Which resembles this earth—its air,
grass, houses, beds, laundry, things to eat—
except that it is articulate,
the accessory, understanding, speaking of
where we are born and love and
move together continually.

Departures are dreams of home,
returns to bodies and minds we're in the habit of.
And what are these terrible things
they are taking for granted? Air and grass,
houses and beds, laundry and things to eat—
so little clarity, so little space between them;
a crowd of distractions to be
bought and done and arranged for,
drugs for the surely incurable pain of
living misunderstood among many who love you.

One evening not long ago
I walked to the high flat stone where,
as children, we used to lie in wait
for the constellations. It was dusk and hazy,
the hills, soft layers of shadow
thick with the scraping of crickets, or katydids,
or whatever you call those shrill unquenchable insects,
sawing their way through night after summer night.
Seated on the stone,
straining into the distance,
it was strangely as if I were
seeing through sound. As if an intensity,
a nagging around me, somehow *became* the mist—
the hills, too, breathing quietly, the sun
quietly falling, disappearing through gauze.

Such seeings have occurred frequently
since we were together. Your quality of perceiving,
a way through, perhaps, or out of, this
damaging anguish. As when we looked down—
you remember that day—into the grassy horse pool
where one bull frog and one crimson maple leaf
quietly brought our hands together.

Dearest, what more can I say?
Here among my chores and my children.
Mine and my husband's children. So many friends.
And in between, these incredible perspectives,
openings entirely ours in the eddying numbness
where, as you know, I am waiting for you
continually.

Ruth

From an Asylum:
Kathy Chattle to her mother, Ruth Arbeiter

MAY 2, 1954

THE GOOD SAMARITAN
HOSPITAL
NEW YORK

Mother,

If I am *where* I am
because I am *what* I am
will you forgive me?

God knows I have fought you long enough ...
soft puppet on the knuckles of your conscience, or
dangling puritanical doll made of duty and habit
and terror and self-revulsion.
At what cost
keeping balance on invisible threads?
At what price
dancing in a sweater set and pearls
on the stage sets of your expectations?

Yes she was a nice girl!
Yes she was good!
Got married. Had a baby.
Just as she should.

Her head was made of walnut
His body of wood.
Then they had a little baby
made of flesh and blood.

Oh mother, poor mother!
Daddy thinks I'm wicked.
Here they think I'm crazy.
Please think I'm dead.

Dead, yes, and watching
from that safe, safe distance.
There. Your stubborn shoulders.

Tight smile.
Head in relief, tilted a little,

74

tense with controlling intelligence.
How can I make you believe
I am myself—a self—
only when dying alive?
Without some interior self-murder
I am blank, void.
The face which I know must be watching
but is never there.
To the flow, you might say, of my experience
what a screen is to the flow of a film.

When I had little Libby, yes,
I was almost real.
But used. Used up.
Almost killed, being able to feel.
'Motherhood will settle her nerves,'
Daddy said, who was never a mother.
I knew in the coil of my head
how I hated her! Hated her!

Christ, how she howled!
And nothing I could feed her . . .
my milk, canned milk, powdered milk, goat's milk . . .
nothing would soothe her.
The doctor? Sympathetic but busy
And I, pouring breastmilk and blood . . .
uncontainable tears . . .
Once, in a quiet hour, I wrote to you.
Frank burned the letter.

He had begun to be gnawed.
Fine unseen teeth were
gnawing him, whittling him.
Wife
forcing him into the prison of a family,
Baby
shaping him into the
middle class, money-earning
ulcered American Dad
Frank's maleness, idealism,
self-flattering, easy conceit
never could admit.

Remember when he bought us that
crazy red, ramshackle farmhouse?

Miles out in the used-to-be country?
Well, his sports car, his sideburns,
his scotch tweeds and 2 a.m. barbecues
gave our wife-swapping, beef-eating neighbors
some unthreatening entertainments!

But by that time we were enemies.
By day hardly speaking.
At night, mutual and experienced torturers.
Libby, our principal weapon,
spun helplessly between us.

'Don't take your venom out on the child!'
Frank would yell at me.
Then whisk her out in his M.G.
To the zoo. To the park.
One day he brought her back
bloodied by a swing.
It was late. Dark.
I didn't say anything.
Called the doctor. Made bandages.
Filled up on whisky.
Later on, both drunk,
he threw me down the cellar stairs,
'Slut!' he kept shouting.
'Slovenly, drunken bitch!'
Which was close to the truth.
I never could live with my life
unless I was drunk.
I never could sleep or cry
until I was drunk.
I drank all day.

One week Frank went away,
just one of his conferences,
and Libby came down with 'flu. A fever.
But she wasn't that sick.
Just sick enough to slash nerves into strips.
Moaning and vomiting
whining and bullying . . .
Panic like a hornet in my brain.
Even my diet of whisky couldn't keep me sane.
No. Don't you tell me she's only a baby.
You know as well as I do, dear,
that babies have selfish grown

bitch personalities curled up in them,
like molars or hair.
When she screamed
she knew she made me scream.
And when I screamed,
she knew I screamed guilt.
Mother! Can't you feel what I felt?
I had to get out of there.
For her sake. For her sake. I ...
Mother, I wished she would die.

So I slept myself sober.
Installed my crone baby-sitter.
Drove to the station.
Took the first train.

It was one of those days when
April is like October. Rain
through a wind full of
knife-edged, excitable sunlight.

Walking from Central Station
feeling slenderer, blonder ...
familiar shiver of pleasure when
men stopped to stare.
Sky again! Younger.
Too scared to go to bars,
wandering like a schoolgirl from
museum to museum ...

The Modern Art. The Guggenheim.
The Frick. The Metropolitan.
At the end, in the end
to the Cloisters.
You took me there often as a child,
you remember? Your small puzzled
prudish fat daughter!

But weirdly, mother, weirdly,
this time it was just as before.
Just as hallowed and hushed and mysterious.
Just as drenched in its greyness and gentleness.
As if I'd been waiting there somewhere,
some part of me waiting in childhood,
expecting myself to come back.

There was one chapel . . .
Crouched, resigned, half-caryatids,
shouldering the arches like sins . . .
on the altar, stiff, under a baldachin,
a statue, a crude wooden Mary
dangling her homunculus son.

She was worn, wormeaten,
hunched in the vestiges of drapery.
Her features? Weary.
Weary and purposeless with suffering.
Her face? Void. A wound of
perpetual suffering.

And she stared at me, down at me,
suffering, out of one
glazed terrible eye.
I took in that gaze like a blade!
What was it? A threat or a lie?
Or did she know?
Her thin Christ had no head!
But did she know?

I don't know what I did,
or why. It blurs now, but I
woke up to find myself here
where they've taken my belt and my
wedding ring, where they
specialize in keeping me weeping.

Come when you can, or when
the whitecoats let you.
But they may not let you, of course.
They think you're to blame.
Good God, mother, I'm not insane!
How can I get out of here?
Can't you get me out of here?

I'll try, I'll try, really,
I'll try again. The marriage.
The baby. The house. The whole damn bore!

Because for me, what the hell else is there?
Mother, what more? What more?

78

Mrs. Lillian Culick, divorcée, to Dr. Frank Chattle

THE CENTRE FOR RESEARCH IN
URBANIZED HUMAN BEHAVIOR
DEPARTMENT OF SOCIAL PSYCHOLOGY
MAY 21, 1954   BLYTHNESS COLLEGE, NEW YORK

Darling,
Or may I still, Frank?
Or should I kneel?
'Sir.' 'Dr. Chattle.'
so . . . salutations from your patient
patient. Anyway, be
decent, dear, and don't destroy me
yet, although you're livid,
I just know it,
at the lie of this
departmental envelope.
But I've tried to write, to
phone so often, Frank, each
empty, echoing evening.
Even if we're through
it's unmanly not to
meet me, not to discuss
us, not to confess.

Does this purposeful burying of
reasons mean you're
banking on a bust-up Frank?
Won't you take a share
of the blame? Well,
I don't know what game
you were playing, but I swear
Kathy's hangups were never
sparked off by *me*!

Ruth phoned and jabbered on
hours about your kid.
She can't know anything.
She'd forget I was
Pollyanna Sunshine
if she walked in and
found us in bed!

79

                    Oh,
let's skip the shit
honey!
I've been in a mood.
Be nice.
I need you.
To be with.
To talk to.
My depression's come back
and I'm living on Valium.
I can't eat.
I can't talk.
I don't know what I want.

Could it be the cut we've
made in our sex life?
I've got some queer shakes.
I can't chew. I
can't sleep. I'm always so
dizzy with Seconal.

Can't you guess what I want?

Well, it may not be you,
Frank. Yes, damn it, I'm
not sure you'd do
in the long run. Oh, you
talk too much and you
kid around too much. You
let yourself down. You know
I never wanted us to be
lovers in the first place!

But I think you understand me.
Won't you make me happy?
Remember what you wrote
about my bones?
I love your little poem
about my bones and my
muscles like dolphins,
and the sea life in the
tides of my skin.

I'll not whet your appetite because
I *don't* know what I want.

So don't come.
Not tonight, anyhow.
Perhaps I'll drop in
at your office tomorrow.
I could do with a
prescription.
I'm all nerves
and I can't swallow.
I've lost five
pounds out of guilt!
(I wish there were some
safe pills for guilt.)

Oh Frank.
Have you felt what
I've felt?
Will you forgive me?
For this letter?
For this agony?
Don't be angry.
I've been lonely.
Let's try to meet soon.
                    OK?

End of a summer's day:
From the journal of Ruth Arbeiter

JUNE, 1968

Dreaming or dying? The room as usual.
Ceiling and woodwork, whites of a calm grey eye.
Curtains in motion. Membranes between myself and the
screaming of the locust. Bed-cage. Locker.
Aluminium pitcher and tray. Neil in the guest chair,
his bought flowers like blood spots.
Why carnations in rose season? Habit.
No, kindness. No, habit of kindness.
An artificial smell all the same.

As when waiting for Father in that hot
hellish hospital in Cambridge after Jimmy died.
Jimmy. Would be now fifty . . . nine. At twenty
a comedian. Grotesque, all nose and glasses, fuzz for hair.
Poor mother's two-hundred-brush-stroke Sundays . . .
still it would never lie down. 'Ruthie,' he whispered,
'run back and fetch me my specs, there's a sister,
and a morning paper.' That between the night's operation
and at noon being dead. Mother at her best brave, praying.
Phil gone for Dad. I, bulky, alone, eighteen,
in the aseptic corridor, hating that I was hungry.
'I am selfish,' I thought, crying about that.
'I can't be unhappy enough.'

College days. Ohio in the nineteen-twenties.
It might just as well have been the nineteenth century.
Our philosophy reconciling Christ and Darwin.
Our Modern Lit embarrassed by Wilde. In those days,
those sandwich days before the Crash I hardly noticed,
before Belgium and Pearl Harbor and Auschwitz—
senseless un-American disasters which destroyed, but
never touched me. Left me a litter of conveniences.
My life. Our double life, poor Neil's and mine,
in Boston, in Cambridge . . . Harvard's Cambridge . . .
so many brilliant, miserable, significant people.

They would have frightened you, Dad, who followed,
stumbling, in the footsteps of your Maker . . .
His footprints too deep for you. Your hurt face peering over.
Dear Dad, dear failure, dear
specialist in injured feelings!
Did you guess how we lived on our tip toes,
towards the end of it, Mother and I?
Every purchase a crisis. Every meal a negotiation.
While you waded away in the swamp of your complaints,
telling everyone that everyone was against you until
everyone *was* against you, and they took you away,
blind, sick and mad, a disquieting absence at my wedding.

Amazing. It is amazing.
Your face. Very clear.
Can you see me? Can you hear me?
I know that, like me, you intended to live a long time.
You admired old age and its accumulation of understanding.
You looked forward to seeing me, half mother,

half Virgin, surrounded by the halo of your grandchildren.
Borne aloft, perhaps, by hundreds of little children!

There. That locust again.
Insect anguish stretched past the limits of restraint.
Jet scream through the blue above the lake.
June and July.
The Children in the rock pits, bristling with tin spades.
They called it 'The Fortress' that crevice in the boulder
where Kathy—in her red striped jersey—and Eden—always
skinny, bony, shivering—played and played.

The wind up suddenly.
                              'Time to pack up now.'
                                             'Ohhhhhhhhhhh!'
a wail in chorus. 'Please, Mommy, one last swim, Mommy!'
'One. Then we go.'

Nicholas, his sunburned body curled hot on my thigh,
is asleep still, in his blind skin.
But the girls splash in carelessly as frogs.
The waves flutter.
The little moored boats, each doubled by the lake,
loosen their masts across the querulous water.

Of course, this is the loss that you prepared me to
prepare for, Paul. That June and July.
Waking beside you at no hour ... leaning for love over
rare wine gone sour in the glasses ... ashtrays spilling over
into books we were never able to get to the end of ...
nights we were never able to get to the end of ...
love into sleep and sleep into love again,
telling time by a laughable hunger or the
slow spreading path of the sun in the dust, on the wallpaper.

Dearest Paul. Suppose we had gone back ... or on.
Would it have been different?
Would you have changed us all?

The question ceases to matter before the question is resolved.

I think I must have thought too often of your thoughts.
Whether of me, or, more likely of your new book ...
unfinished. Like your life, unfinished.
Never begun, really, never committed to anything so

83

self-defining as a name, a place, a family . . . anything
that might twist the eddying possibilities
into a frame around you. Not a failure, like Father.
Not a liar like myself . . . who finds, not you, but this
usual earth strange to take leave of.

PART THREE
Living for Now

Professor Arbeiter to his dead wife

AUGUST, 1968   CLEARFIELD, VERMONT

The worst time is waking
                as if every nerve were working
scalpels in the running wound, knives in the gash.
For in life, love, nothing begins or ends with a clean crash.
The brain knows, but habit is like cash or clothes.
It continues its momentum like a blind weight through glass.

I can't lie down in the dark with your severed voice, Ruth.
In this room full of trivial attentions I am still your guest.
'You're cold, dear. Let me fetch you your rug.'
'You're tired, I know. I'll tell them you need to rest.'
  Here. Again. On the phone. Overheard in the hall,
'I'm sorry. My husband is working. At seven? I'll tell him you
    called.'

Ruth, in our thirty-eight years lost to eye-strain and bad temper
you never spoke to me once of what I know.
I neither dared nor dared not to speak to you, though
sometimes your inattentions drove black words like swarming
    insects
swimming in held-back tears through my desperate paragraphs.

I was proud of you, Ruth. My girl.
My critic. My helpmate. Hostess to a pack of fools
you could always smile at. Confidante of students
too shy to seek me out. Friend of all milkmen and maids.
One day, one June, you gave tea to Isaiah Berlin.
                  And invited our Clearfield carpenter.

These last years have been . . . what, Ruth?

Living with someone who's dying. Not letting her know.
And she, although not told, knowing.
As though the courtesy of our mutual lie

85

were drawing us together under its canopy.
I read to you. Henry Adams. You had so much to say.
You asked for a handkerchief the last day. Impatiently.
            As if death were a head cold.

I dream most nights of a garden. Formal. Like Versailles.
Laid out in terraces, box hedges, sculptured old
gods and goddesses.
                        We are walking together on a gravel path
when suddenly the vista changes. Frames of ash
are descending in geometrical patterns
                                    to a dry fountain.

But worst is waking.
Reaching for the radio through the strings of your voice.
Listening to the whining of hillbillies, over and over.
            Closing my eyes
        as if the night could never be over.

Nick Arbeiter writes poems on the road to Wyoming after a funeral in Vermont

JULY–AUGUST, 1968

I

(*Albany*)
West, man, West.
                I'm being fed to my own bogged veins!
Know yourself. Your inheritance.
Self-hating. Self-abasing.
                How we eat of ourselves!
'Just the family,' Father said.
                                Death was real.

Then the crows flocked in
                        trained for crises,
to deck out a flesh corpse like waxwork,
to croak hoarse Amens to a long box,
to peck out old photographs.

86

Christ thought he could sell us the strait gate
                    if we paid him in sacrifice,
if we gave up the apple of knowledge
                    for his extraordinary wine.

But Christ's Presbyterian blood for her was grapejuice.
His narrow gates opened to the total wind.

I remember they made her smile
for the earth seeping in
                    through the aisles of her abandoned body,
        eroding it,   book and pew.

II

(*Akron*)
Waking up every morning in a different city
which is always the same city in a different place
with always the same woman sprawled adrift in the sheets
as if lost in the confusing surfaces of her names . . .

how soft it feels floating up through the old gauze places.
Hollyhocks and blue wallpaper,   stones,   resonances,
                    window-glass watery as a lake.

Two little girls and a woman reflected among the bright leaves.
They shimmer there inverted in a glaze crimson as sumac.
They are beautiful,   they smile at me,   they invite me to
    drown.

Now an air conditioner bores me with monotonous stories.
A window, flowered with curtains, frames me a Greek façade.
That strip of red neon must have been left on all night.
It flashes mechanically. VACANCIES   VACANCIES.

My last night's girl shrouds her breasts,   moans for coffee.
Doors slam in the dew-drenched cars.
                            Their engines start up.

III

(*Scotts Bluff*)
In Nebraska it's the moon.
Mario's Steakhouse and Bar in the middle of the moon.
Ramshackle leftover, left over U.S. 20.   102 Fahrenheit.
                    Clay   wind   and sand.

87

The dry waves in rings around the wrecks of meteorites.
Slabs of eroded igneous. Tongues out at the stars.

Tonight there is empty thunder over the white bandage of the
    highway.
Occasional cars are missiles, are implorers.
Voices wailing to rain gods locked in the dry horizons.

Walking in crimson dusk or in scalding wind.
Wading through the sediment of ages cleft for no one,
these are the world's negations. This is the wilderness.

Scotts Bluff. Bleaching like a relic in the North Platte's
wandering incision in the dead sheet of the Plains.
Pleistocene valleys rucked up in raw clay, claws
reaching to root out and tear up all inhabitants and habitations.
Jaws incisors unappeased by city names ...
Jail Rock and *Smokestack Roundhouse* and *Twin Sisters*.
They will not be made flesh. They will not accept parables.

The dry creeks are shot thick with millennial flints,
with the dust of the dog-sized horses of the dust of Pawnees.

IV

They say to you
    whatever is in your mind.
        The white sands.

V

(*Laramie*)
At every motel the formica boys
        swagger in with their chromium girlfriends.
The restaurant rocks as the juke box slings out
        hits from a two-years-stale menu.

I smoke in a corner booth, take in the floor show.
The girls with their leathery eyelashes and fringed thighs.
The boys with their low-slung belts, their sharpened shoes.
'Let it be, let it be' and rock-a-bye baby, Daddy.

You taught us discretion in a woman
             was worth all the dollars in Hollywood.
No one could have bought you equipment to play your own wife.

We knew her moods like the roads in our New England county.
You knew her like a map
                    you could depend on to get to your destination.

VI

Palms up cupping the globe of his twelve-year-old cognac,
Father reminisced and accused himself.
Neighbors called on tiptoe, bearing jam and casseroles.
Bald Maxwell quoted Keats and got drunk.

'When I think of the waste, the sheer waste,' Father maundered.
'And with so much to give and to live for . . .'

'She gave us her light,' agreed Maxwell.
'She burned out her love for more of us than she could afford to.'

VII

It's dangerous to live in a noose of 'I want' and 'I ought'.
Antaeus, held too high by Hercules, broke his root to the soil.
Our race thins. We're second growths
                        fighting for what's left of the sky.

VII

We accuse you, fathers,
                    we accuse you of lies,
of pouring out a smoke screen
                    of high-minded fervor,
and then setting off to murder
                    under twin banners, Profit and
                                        Compromise.

We accuse you of signing on
                    with Corporation Hypocrisy,
of willing us a money machine
                    that feeds us by consuming us like fuel,
of letting cities rule
                    while the grass withers and the
rivers pullulate with acids,
                    of setting up houses like music boxes where

love is only wound up once
                and then allowed to run down.
We accuse you of using reason
                    to sanction massacre,
of making freedom
                a one way street with barbed wire.
We accuse you of not understanding
                even now why you are what you are,
though under the asphalt
                there rises a burning savage
and over his ashes
                you glide in a soft mirage.
Will you have time to hear us
                who go easy and barefoot?
who are earthbound in airports?
                who are flesh among cars?
Will you give us your deserts
                and let us bring life there?
Will you watch us making love
                between your carports and skyscrapers?

We are weak.
        We are human.
                We are unsure.
We train our few possessions
        to stand under us like ankles.
We like dreams.
        We like trips.
                We've got a Hell you've never been to.
Black or white,
                men are miracles to us.
Sick or poor,
                truth is sustenance to us.
Waking or dreaming
                they're the same thing to us.
So that there be peace among the animals.

Epilogue:
Kay Boyd to her father, Professor Arbeiter

JULY 4, 1972   HAVERSTOCK HILL,
                                LONDON, N.W.3.

Dearest Father,

This is the anniversary of our loss.
I write to the shushing of trees outside my window
(London planes, sycamores in Massachusetts)
watching them sift light restlessly on a tiny garden.
The leaves are palm-shaped, like New England maples,
but the wind drags them aside like a loose drapery
as if trying to expose some savage or gipsy origin.

Our maples never stooped to be voluptuous.
They were prim New England. Trim domes. Upright clouds.

Yes, leaves sweep away from the trunks of these English trees
the way mist lifts from her farms.
The bark is like topographical shading
Or the shadings of accent and stone in this wrinkled country.

'Come back,' Eden wrote, after mother died.
'Come help me to keep her alive a little longer.'

But I didn't go back because I couldn't see what to come back to.
I couldn't think who to go back as.
That Kathy my name was, that Mrs. Frank Chattle
died in New York of divorce.
Kay Boyd, the woman, the writer, has survived.
She lives a long way from Eden. The tug back
is allegiance to innocence which is not there.

'In the floodtides of *Civitas Mundi*
New England is dissolving like a green chemical.
Old England bleeds out to meet it in mid-ocean.
          Nowhere is safe.'

It is a poem I can't continue.
It is America I can't contain.

Dear Father, I love but can't know you.
    I've given you all that I can.
    Can these pages make amends for what was not said?
    Do justice to the living, to the dead?

ENOUGH OF GREEN

To Write It

You must always be alone.
But don't beg a soupscrap of charity
or birdcrumb of tolerance.
Shift for yourself.
As furniture heaves off your life
you'll love your deliverance.

Until loneliness slips in, scrawny
and hungry, Miss Loneliness, over the
barrenness, bribing with company.
Restlessness, one of her attendants.
And the drunk twins, of course,
Memory and Remorse.

Refuse them. Stay faithful to Silence, just
Silence, sliding between that breath
and now this breath, severing the tick
from the tock on the alarm clock,
measuring the absence of else.
And the presence, the privilege.

The Sun Appears in November

When trees are bare,
when ground is more glowing than summer,
in sun, in November,
you can see what lay under
confusing eloquence of green.

Bare boughs in their cunning
twist this way and that way
trying to persuade by crooked reasoning.
But trees are constrained from within
to conform to skeleton.

Nothing they put on
will equal these lines of cold branches,
the willows in bunches,
birches like lightning,
transparent in brown spinneys, beeches.

North Sea off Carnoustie

For Jean Rubens

You know it by the northern look of the shore,
by the salt-worried faces,
by an absence of trees, an abundance of lighthouses.
It's a serious ocean.

Along marram-scarred, sandbitten margins
wired roofs straggle out to where
a cold little holiday fair
has floated in and pitched itself
safely near the prairie of the golf course.
Coloured lights are sunk deep into the solid wind,
but all they've caught is a pair of lovers
and three silly boys.
Everyone else has a dog.
Or a room to get to.

The smells are of fish and of sewage and cut grass.
Oystercatchers, doubtful of habitation,
clamour 'weep, weep, weep' as they fuss over
scummy black rocks the tide leaves for them.

The sea is as near as we come to another world.

But there in your stony and windswept garden
a blackbird is confirming the grip of the land.
'You, you,' he murmurs, dark purple in his voice.

And now in far quarters of the horizon
lighthouses are awake, sending messages—
invitations to the landlocked,
warnings to the experienced,
but to anyone returning from the planet ocean,
candles in the windows of a safe earth.

Fire and the Tide

Fire struggles in the chimney like an animal.
It's caught in a life,
as when the tide pulls the Tay out
scarring predictable mudscape—
seawater's knifework
notching quick runnel and channel.

That's how you remember
the alternative lives.
You saw them, could never have lived them.
A ribbon of birds is pulled raggedly over November.
You're pulled between now and the way you will not escape.

The Mudtower

And again, without snow, a new year.
As for fifty years, a thousand years, the air
returns the child-blue rage of the river.
Six swans rise aloud from the estuary,
ferrying tremendous souls to the pond by the playground.
They're coming for me! No. I'm a part of the scenery.
They fly low, taking no interest in migratory ladies.

The stone town stumbles downhill to untidy mudflats—
high square houses, shivering in windows, the street of shops,
the church and clocktower, school, the four worn pubs
artfully spaced between dry rows of cottages.
Then council flats, fire station, rusty gasometer,
timber yard baying out its clean smell of pinewood.
Then grass, swings, mud. The wilted estuary.

You could say that the winter's asleep in the harbour's arm.
Two sloops with their heads on their backs are sleeping there
                                        peacefully.

Far out in the tide's slum, in the arm of the sand-spit,
the mudtower wades in the giving and taking water.

Its uses—if it ever had uses—have been abandoned.
The low door's a mouth. Slit eyes stab the pinnacle.
Its lovethrust is up from the mud it seems to be made of.
Surely it's alive and hibernating, Pictish and animal.
The sea birds can hear it breathing in its skin or shrine.

How those lighthouses, airing their bones on the coast,
hate the mudtower! They hold their white messages aloft
like saints bearing scriptures.

As the water withdraws, the mudtower steps out on the land.
Watch the fierce, driven, hot-looking
scuttlings of redshanks, the beaks of the oystercatchers.
Struggle and panic. Struggle and panic.
Mud's rituals resume. The priest-gulls flap to the kill.
Now high flocks of sandpipers, wings made of sunlight,
flicker as snow flickers, blown from those inland hills.

With my Sons at Boarhills

Gulls think it is for them
that the wormy sand rises,
brooding on its few rights,
losing its war with water.

The mussel flats ooze out,
and now the barnacled, embossed
stacked rocks are pedestals for strangers,
for my own strange sons,
scraping in the pool,
imperilling their pure reflections.

Their bodies are less beautiful than
blue heaven's pleiades of herring gulls,
or gannets, or that sloop's sail
sawtoothing the sea as if its
scenery were out of date, as if its
photographs had all been taken:
two boys left naked in a sloughed off summer,
skins and articulate backbones,
fossils for scrapbook or cluttered mantelpiece.

If you look now, quickly and askance,
you can see how the camera's eye
perfected what was motion and chance before
it clicked on this day and childhood snapshot,
scarcely seen beside
hunched rugby stripes and ugly uniforms—
shy, familiar grins in a waste of faces.

My knee joints ache and crack
as I kneel to my room's fire, feeding it.
Steam wreathes from my teacup, clouding
the graduate, the lieutenant, the weddings,
the significant man of letters, the politician
smiling from his short victory . . .

Faces I washed and scolded, only
watched as my each child laboured from his own womb,
bringing forth, without me, men who must
call me mother, love or reassess me
as their barest needs dictate, return
dreaming, rarely to this saltpool in memory,
naked on a morning full of see-through jellyfish,
with the tide out and the gulls out
grazing on healed beaches,
while sea-thrift blazes by the dry path,
and the sail stops cutting the water to pieces
and heads for some named port inland.

Their voices return like footprints over the sandflats,
permanent, impermanent, salt and sensuous
as the sea is, in its frame, its myth.

The Exhibition

For Alasdair Gray

The exhibition is of
   all the exhibited people
      gathered together at the exhibition.

How pleasing. Everyone is at ease.
   The canvasses are amiably walking around
      choosing faces which are

cut out of smooth brown packing paper,
   pasted meticulously in the spaces
      wearing their names.

How can they fail to be flattered,
   these figures who, in frames,
      stay distressingly apart from one another,

but when meeting themselves on the walls
   are so delighted?
      That woman lying naked on the bed,

for instance, stops
   brooding over her weakness of will
      and admires her thighs.

And the man without shoes, in his necktie,
   approves his cool sense of detachment,
      his power to despatch it and rise.

Yes, it's all satisfactory self-fulfilment—
   admirer and admired so embraced
      there's no place for the past,

though behind both paint and gallery
   you can see that some old city is
      thinning to dissolution.

Distances between shoulder and shoulder
   and eye and eye grow wider as the
      waste lots fill up with workers'

rubble: brokenhearts, hangovers, torn sheets,
   yards of mattress stuffing, bottles,
      cigarette butts, used newspapers.

Enlightened, momentarily spared,
   the invited say 'thank you' and
      go in their separate directions.

Now the pictures, left holding their
   bodies and heads, have no chance of
      changing things at all by making connections.

Night Wind, Dundee

At sundown, a seaforce that gulls rode or fell through.
The small snow is surf. Eddies of strong air
swarm up old tenements. Listen! My window's
late rat-tat-tat guns back at who and whose enemy
milked the sky's agates, polished its ebony.
Warm rooms are lit up in bare blocks of concrete.
Someone's ripped cobwebs from a great vault's rafters,
revealing a moonface, a starfield,
barbarian Orion crucified in God's heaven.

Aberdeen

Old daughter with a rich future,
that's blueveined Aberdeen,
reeking of fish, breathing sea air
like atomized pewter. Her clean
gothic ribs rattle protests to the
spiky gusts. Poor girl.
She's got to marry oil.
Nobody who loves her wants to save her.

Ragwort

They won't let railways alone, those yellow flowers.
They're that remorseless joy of dereliction
darkest banks exhale like vivid breath
as bricks divide to let them root between.
How every falling place concocts their smile,
taking what's left and making a song of it.

By the Boat House, Oxford

They belong here in their own quenched country.
I had forgotten nice women could be so nice,
smiling beside large sons on the makeshift quay,
frail, behind pale faces and hurt eyes.

Their husbands are plainly superior, with them, without them.
Their boys wear privilege like a clear inheritance, easily.
(Now a swan's neck couples with its own reflection,
making in the simple water a perfect 3.)

The punts seem resigned to an unexciting mooring.
But the women? It's hard to tell. Do their fine grey hairs
and filament lips approve or disdain the loving
that living alone, or else lonely in pairs, impairs?

A Summer Place

You know that house she called home,
so sleek, so clapboard-white,
that used to be some country jobber's blight
or scab on our hill's arm.
You can see the two cellars of the barn,
stones still squatting where the fellow stacked them.

He worked the place as a farm,
though how, with stones for soil, she never knew.
Partly she hoped he'd been a poet, too—
why else hang Haystack mountain and its view
from north-west windows?
It was the view she bought it for. He'd gone.
The house sagged on its frame. The barns were down.

The use she saw for it was not to be
of use. A summer place. A lovely
setting where fine minds could graze
at leisure on long summer days
and gather books from bushes, phrase by phrase.
Work would be thought. A tractor bought for play
would scare unnecessary ugly scrub away.

A white gem set on a green silk glove
she bought and owned there.
And summers wore it, just as she would wear
each summer like a dress of sacred air
until the house was half compounded of
foundations, beams and paint, half of her love.

She lived profoundly, felt, wrote from her heart,
knew each confessional songbird by its voice,
cloistered her garden with bee balm and fanning iris,
sat, stained by sunsets, in a vault of noise
listening through cricket prayer for whitethroat,
hermit thrush—and couldn't keep it out,
the shade of something wrong, a fear, a doubt,

as though she heard the house stir in its plaster,
stones depart unsteadily from walls,
the woods, unwatched, stretch out their roots like claws
and tear through careful fences, fiercer than saws.
Something alive lived under her mind-cropped pasture,
hated the house—or worse, loved, hungering after
its perfectly closed compactness, breathed disaster.

She dreamed or daydreamed what it might have come to,
the house itself, wanting the view
to take it, and the view's love gathering into
brambles, tendrils, trunks of maples, needing
her every window, entering, seeding . . .
Fear of attack kept her from sleeping,
kept her awake in her white room, pacing, weeping.

But you see the place still stands there, pretty as new.
Whatever she thought the mountain and trees would do,
they did—and took her with them—and withdrew.

Thales and Li Po

Thales, out
scanning the stars for truth,
walked into a well.
Li Po fell in love
with the moon's
reflection
in the Yellow River.

Which was the right way to die?
It doesn't matter.
Try an analysis of sky, or
passionate, ignorant,
embrace a lie.

The Price

The fear of loneliness, the wish
to be alone;
love grown rank as seeding grass
in every room,
and anger at it, raging at it,
storming it down.

Also that four-walled chrysalis
and impediment, home;
that lamp and hearth, that easy fit
of bed to bone;
those children, too, sharp witnesses
of all I've done.

My dear, the ropes that bind us
are safe to hold;
the walls that crush us keep us
from the cold.
I know the price and still I pay it, pay it—
words, their furtive kiss,
illicit gold.

Path

Aged by rains
and cool under pulsing trees,
the summer path is paved with winter leaves.
Roots lace it like an old man's veins.

And nothing in field, on hill, can so appal
burnt August and its transitory walker
as this which leads a summer
towards its fall.

Now under cover
of the leopard pelt
of that lean way, more heat, more passions felt
than ever in shimmering field by usual lover.

Fanged with surprising light, the path means harm.
Not calm, not comfort, not release from love.
White innocent motes of dust
rise up and swarm.

Temporarily in Oxford

Where they will bury me
I don't know.
Many places might not be
sorry to store me.

The Midwest has right of origin.
Already it has welcomed my mother
to its flat sheets.

The English fens that bore me
have been close curiously often.
It seems I can't get away from
dampness and learning.

If I stay where I am
I could sleep in this educated earth.

But if they are kind
they'll burn me and
send me to Vermont.

I'd be an education for the trees
and would relish, really,
flaring into maple each October—
my scarlet letter to you.

Your stormy north is possible.
You will be there, engrossed in its peat.

It would be handy not to have to
cross the whole Atlantic
each time I wanted to
lift up the turf
and slip in beside you.

Cain

Lord have mercy upon the angry.
The anguished can take care of each other.
The angels will take care of themselves.
But the angry have no daughters or mothers;
only brute brothers, I· ... I.
Hearing that faint 'Abel, Abel' they stop their ears.
Watching that approved flame snake to the sky
they beat stubby blades out of ploughshares,
cut the sun out of the air,
stamp on small fires they might have seen by.

Drought

After the exhilaration of the peaks
look on, look back—
infatuations—screes parched to their rock—
a river of dry water scours dry land—
those twisted, black, alluvial obsessions—
memory is a river without rain.

Restore the flood of simple speech again,
the affectionate plash of word thrown over pain,
the brown of perpetual flowing where your hand
thrusts white beneath the cold of sliding waters,
invites, invents, forgives its own distortion,
gripping the green of live and rooted matters.

After the End of It

You gave and gave,
and now you say you're poor.
I'm in your debt, you say,
and there's no way to repay you
but by my giving more.

Your pound of flesh is what you must have?
Here's what I've saved.

This sip of wine is yours,
this sieve of laughter. Yours,
too, these broken haloes
from my cigarette, these coals
that flicker when the salt wind howls
and the letter box blinks like a loud
eyelid over the empty floor.

I'll send this, too, this gale between rains,
this wild day. Its cold is so cold
I want to break it into panes
like new ice on a pond; then pay it
pain by pain to your account.
Let it freeze us both into some numb country!
Giving and taking might be the same there.
A future of measurement and blame
gone in a few bitter minutes.

In the Orchard

Black bird, black voice,
almost the shadow of a voice,
so kind to this tired summer sky,
a rim of night around it,
yet almost an echo of today,
all the days since that first
soft guttural disaster
gave us 'apple' and 'tree'
and all that transpired thereafter
in the city of the tongue.

Blackbird, so old, so young,
happy to be stricken with a song
you can never choose away from.

Resurrection

Surprised by spring,
by the green light fallen like snow
in a single evening,
by hawthorn, blackthorn, willow,

meadow—everything
woken again after how many thousand years?
As if there had been no years.

That generous throat
is a blackbird's. Now, a thrush.
And that ribbon flung out,
that silk voice, is a chaffinch's rush
to his grace-note.
Birds woo, or apportion the innocent air they're made for.
Whom do they sing for?

Old man by the river
spread out like a cross in the sun
feet bare
and stared at by three grubby children,
you've made it again, and yes we'll inherit a summer.
Always the same green clamouring fells you that wakes you.
And you have to start living again when it wakes you.

The Sirens are Virtuous

They are not what you think.
The sirens are virtuous.
Very smart. Very dedicated.
In their true form
ladies. Not women. Not fish.
They abhor boring islands.
But wherever a human vortex is,
there they are at the centre.

'Come unto me, all ye who labour
and are weary without reason
and I will give you
fresh causes of feverish concern,'
sings one, penetrating the plugged ears
of the never-at-rest.

Looking guilty inward
from under the O, slowing swinging
of Ought, these men are terrified—
its noose lowering—

so they witness with relief
its transformation into a mouth.
Lips. Warmth. Breath.
What is it to them
that it is shouting,
not kissing?

The ladies are professionals,
they divide and devour
professionally.
Helmsman from the helm.
Herdsman from the herd.
Though always there is one
who will not peel off and die joyfully,
in a good season
thousands can be loved, sucked,
drained, disposed of.

'There, our laps are full,'
cry the ladies at intervals,
shaking out their skirts,
shaking the bones from their aprons.
'And how we adored them, the drab cockatoos,
the serious darlings, the nearly salvational
whey-faced fellows of feverish concern.'

Minister

We're going to need the minister
to help this heavy body into the ground.

But he won't dig the hole.
Others who are stronger and weaker will have to do that.
And he won't wipe his nose and his eyes.
Others who are weaker and stronger will have to do that.
And he won't bake cakes or take care of the kids—
women's work—anyway,
what would they do at a time like this
if they didn't do that?

No, we'll get the minister to come
and take care of the words.

He doesn't have to make them up.
He doesn't have to say them well.
He doesn't have to like them
so long as they agree to obey him.

We have to have the minister
so the words will know where to go.

Imagine them circling and circling
the confusing cemetery.
Imagine them roving the earth
without anywhere to rest.

Meniscus

The moon at its two extremes,
promise and reminiscence,
future and past succeeding each other,
the rim of a continuous event.

These eyes which contain the moon
in the suspect lens of an existence,
guiding it from crescent to crescent
as from mirror to distorting mirror.

The good bones sheathed in my skin,
the remarkable knees and elbows
working without audible complaint
in the salty caves of their fitting.

My cup overfilled at the brim
and beyond the belief of the brim.
Absolved by the power of the lip
from the necessity of falling.

Respectable House

Worth keeping your foot in the door.
Worth letting the lamplight stripe your shoe
and escape in the dark behind you.

Worth the candle-width of a velvet floor,
the swell of a stair, a tinkle of glasses,
and overheard—rising and flaring—those fortunate voices.

Push open the door. More. And a little more.
You seem to be welcome. You can't help stepping inside.
You see how light and its residents have lied.

You see what the gun on the table has to be used for.

Colours

Enough of green
though to remember childhood
is to stand in uneasy radiance
under those trees.

Enough yellow.
We are looking back
over our shoulders, telling our children
to be happy.

Try to forget about red.
Leave it to the professionals.
But perceive heaven as a density
blue enough to abolish the stars.

As long as the rainbow lasts
the company stays.

Of black there is never enough.

One by one the lights in the house go out.
Step over the threshold. Forget
to take my hand.

MINUTE BY GLASS MINUTE

Swifts

Spring comes little, a little. All April it rains.
The new leaves stick in their fists. New ferns, still fiddleheads.
But one day the swifts are back. Face to the sun like a child
You shout, 'The swifts are back!'

Sure enough, bolt nocks bow to carry one sky-scyther
Two hundred miles an hour across fullblown windfields.
Swreeeee. Swreeee. Another. And another.
It's the cut air falling in shrieks on our chimneys and roofs.

The next day, a fleet of high crosses cruises in ether.
These are the air pilgrims, pilots of air rivers . . .
But a shift of wing and they're earth-skimmers, daggers,
Skilful in guiding the throw of themselves away from
    themselves.

Quick flutter, a scimitar upsweep, out of danger of touch, for
Earth is forbidden to them, water's forbidden to them.
All air and fire, little owlish ascetics, they outfly storms.
They rush to the pillars of altitude, the thermal fountains.

Here is a legend of swifts, a parable—
When the great Raven bent over earth to create the birds
The swifts were ungrateful. They were small muddy things
Like shoes, with long legs and short wings, so

They took themselves off to the mountains to sulk.
And they stayed there. 'Well,' said the Raven, after years of this,
'I will give you the sky, you can have the whole sky
On condition that you give up rest.'

'Yes, yes,' screamed the swifts. 'We abhor rest.
We detest the filth of growth, the sweat of sleep,
Soft nests in the wet fields, slimehold of worms.
Let us be free, be air!'

So the Raven took their legs and bound them into their bodies.
He bent their wings like boomerangs, honed them like knives.
He streamlined their feathers and stripped them of velvet.
Then he released them, *Never to Return*

Inscribed on their feet and wings. And so
We have swifts, though in reality not parables but
Bolts in the world's need, swift
Swifts, not in punishment, not in ecstasy, simply

Sleepers over oceans in the mill of the world's breathing.
The grace to say they live in another firmament.
A way to say the miracle will not occur,
And watch the miracle.

Buzzard and Alder

Buzzard that folds itself into and becomes nude
alder; alder that insensibly becomes bird—
one life inside the dazzling tree. Together
they do change everything, and forever.

You think, because no news is said here,
not. But rain's rained weather to a rare
blue, so you can see the thinness of it,
I mean the layer they live in, flying in it,

breaking through it minute by glass minute.
Buzzard, hunched in disuse before it
shatters winter, wheeling after food.
Alder, silently glazing us, the dead.

Burnished

Walking out of Hay in the rain, imagining Blake
imagining the real world into existence,
I suddenly turned on him and said with energy—
How dare you inflict imagination on us!
What halo does the world deserve? And he—
Let worlds die burnished, as along this bank.

Beautiful, I said to him and to the world's brown
oiled by the cloud still wet in its spiny shell.
A gloss of red horses' flank shone in its name.
To hold, it was a smooth pebble
mountain water had been running over. Sculpted round,
it swam like an embryo in my palm.

Now close your eyes. I felt the whole world warmed.
It was breathing its native heat in my blind skin.
When I looked again, it was a leather ocean
lapping a small sandy island. No one
appeared to live there. Now where its gleam had been
is a breast with a shrivelled nipple, like a dry wound.

Himalayan Balsam

Orchid-lipped, loose-jointed, purplish, indolent flowers,
with a ripe smell of peaches, like a girl's breath through lipstick,
delicate and coarse in the weedlap of late summer rivers,
dishevelled, weak-stemmed, common as brambles, as love which

subtracts us from seasons, their courtships and murders,
(*Meta segmentata* in her web, and the male waiting,
between blossom and violent blossom, meticulous spiders
repeated in gossamer, and the slim males waiting . . .)

Fragrance too rich for keeping, too light to remember,
like grief for the cat's sparrow and the wild gull's
beach-hatched embryo. (She ran from the reaching water
with the broken egg in her hand, but the clamped bill

refused brandy and grubs, a shred too naked and perilous for
life offered freely in cardboard boxes, little windowsill
coffins for bird death, kitten death, squirrel death, summer
repeated and ended in heartbreak, in the sad small funerals.)

Sometimes, shaping bread or scraping potatoes for supper,
I have stood in the kitchen, transfixed by what I'd call love
if love were a whiff, a wanting for no particular lover,
no child, or baby or creature. 'Love, dear love'

I could cry to these scent-spilling ragged flowers
and mean nothing but 'no', by that word's breadth,
to their evident going, their important descent through red
    towering
stalks to the riverbed. It's not, as I thought, that death

creates love. More that love knows death. Therefore
tears, therefore poems, therefore the long stone sobs of
    cathedrals
that speak to no ferret or fox, that prevent no massacre.
(I am combing abundant leaves from these icy shallows.)

Love, it was you who said, 'Murder the killer
we have to call life and we'd be a bare planet under a dead sun.'
Then I loved you with the usual soft lust of October
that says 'yes' to the coming winter and a summoning odour of
    balsam.

A Bad Day Wants to be Born

A blotched wet morning in Wales that is steamy summer.
Dissolved, my dream of frost melting on grass,
a green wave catching a wet field's iceblades, glass.
Something good there wanted to be lost.

A cow stands thoroughly by her sick calf,
sagged by her udder; the swinging pink vat
sweeps aside pink campion. Even my cat
knows more about death than I do.

And her kitten of three weeks knew
exactly how to take itself out of the
litter on wild rickety legs, to die
privately. Dignity is animal,

is this cold mole's perfect leather hands,
the white nails. I feel that possible flaw
between us open its huge earth jaw.
Do we have to shout across it

or can we reach? I would like not
to go down into the rift again alone.
I would like this day not to be born.
Love, don't talk to me. Hold me.

Pennine

Hills? Or a high plateau scissored by rivers?
Strong as grass, a winter's crop of stones
Craters the drive. The black paths trickle.
Randomly, fells erupt in armoured cliffs
That might be houses—might, in this cloud, be
Slack, grit, slag, moss, a memory of mills.

Everything trains to the perpendicular.
Trees stand taller on one green root than another.
The village is slabbed like steps into its slope,
Its churchyard paved with graves, thronged with unbalanced
Mitred headstones, an asylum of bishops. The dead
Are unsafe. Their graves hardly hold them.

Victorian conscience breathes over church and ruin
A slatey rain. Whoever sent a dove
To star the cross where Thomas Holinrake's buried
Guessed that its message needed marble.
Feathers and blood stab at the lichened walls,
Stonefalls crossing in their long decline.

If I Could Paint Essences

Another day in March. Late
rawness and wetness. I hear my mind say,
if only I. could paint essences . . .

such as the mudness of mud
on this rainsoaked dyke where coltsfoot
displays its yellow misleading daisy;

such as the westness of west here
in England's last thatched, rivered
county. Red ploughland. Green pasture.

Black cattle. Quick water. Overpainted
by lightshafts from layered gold
and purple cumulus. A cloudness of clouds

which are not like anything but clouds.

114

But just as I arrive at true sightness of seeing,
unexpectedly I want to play on those bell-toned
cellos of delicate not-quite-flowering larches

that offer on the opposite hill their unfurled
amber instruments—floating, insubstantial, a rising
horizon of music embodied in light.

And in such imaginings I lose sight of sight.
Just as I will lose the tune of what
hurls in my head, as I turn back, turn

home to you, conversation, the inescapable ache
of trying to catch, say, the catness of cat
as he crouches, stalking his shadow,

on the other side of the window.

From the Men of Letters

How lucky we are
to have a room in language. We
who are known take pride in our hotel.

Naturally
the unknown want to be us, but
they are crippled.

All of us are crippled, but
they are most crippled whose
disasters encourage our art.

They live
swarming and unnamed
in the rubble of a moment.

We live
decently rehoused
in the storeys of a time.

When they throw their arms
around our words
and weep

we are horribly embarrassed.
How will their experience
forgive our tall books?

He and It

(A pathetic fantasy)

This world is not *it*, he felt.
Something is missing.
Impatiently as day pressed into the west
he waited for it to be embers.
Swans churning water in the ordinary river
he wanted to be women or gods,
and when boughs of the competent willows
lost their pure neuter droop and
he saw they were miserables weeping,
he couldn't prevent himself thinking,
'What is missing is me.'

Nothing complained when he drew the world
gently through the narrows of his need
till it cradled his head.

How comfortably it fits the creator
is what he describes.
From his helmet of globe he declares
that sky burns, wind bites,
swans hound him with meaning.
Nevertheless (his voice sounds
a little faint now)
he knows he isn't losing.
He relies on his friend the sun
to beam him messages of light.

He allows the stars to be hopeful
when he winks them at night.
He likes their eyes.

Small Philosophical Poem

Dr Animus, whose philosophy is a table,
sits down contentedly to a square meal.
The plates lie there, and there,
just where they should lie.
His feet stay just where they should stay,
between legs and the floor.
His eyes believe the clean waxed surfaces
are what they are.

But while he's eating his un-
exceptional propositions, his wise
wife Anima, sweeping a haze-gold decanter
from a metaphysical salver,
pours him a small glass of doubt.
Just what he needs.
He smacks his lips and cracks his knuckles.
The world is the pleasure of thought.

He'd like to stay awake all night
(elbows on the table)
talking of how the table might not be there.
But Anima, whose philosophy is hunger,
perceives the plates are void in empty air.
The floor is void beneath his trusting feet.
Peeling her glass from its slender cone of fire
she fills the room with love. And fear. And fear.

Ah Babel

your tower allures me—
its lettered battlements,
sounds, words,
but the high forehead unfinished.

I would desert my eyes
for the windows that are you.

Your multiple stones
despise clouds.
Your country's bleached sand
and black scars

lead to a sky
as clean as meaning.

Nameless
in mist and silence,
grey against grey,
I exist in your promise,

praise you for this present
of a vast home,
pronounced ruin,
all that is known.

Lockkeeper's Island

It is late, but as usual
we will turn away from sleep
and follow the river.

The houses will withdraw as usual,
seeming to be blind.
The path will seem more dangerous,
flooded with shadows,

crossing the narrow footbridge
over the slipstream,
crossing the inflicted hurry of the weir,
crossing to the lockkeeper's
gated, moated island

meeting the river's divided darkness there.

We will not talk at all, but as usual
my hand will say to yours,
'A river in the middle of an island
is that island's island, alien element,
daring the tedium of the safe.'

You'll observe, under Orion,
how an island at the centre of a river
is like the pupil of an eye.

Everything will be silent on the island
except for the sliding water.
The lockkeeper will be sleeping.
His dog, his wife, his name, his discontents—
they will be silent and asleep.

Only the eye will be awake as usual,
keeping watch on the source,
keeping open the vein of the sea's
dangerous protection,

wild water, out-poured, sluiced forth,
declaring this winter one island between
summer and summer, this night, one island
in the archipelago of nights, this city,
one perilous island set lightly on gold
quivering pillars of itself.

Above the lockkeeper's island,
the absolute moon—bright stone,
dry island among inaccessible islands—
will drag its magnet,
make its connections.

Between moon and water,
the consoling machinery of the land.

No moon will bless this place,
or the houses on it,
or this black latticework of derricks,
or these bridges shadowed by trains,
their argument with darkness.

'Blessing' is a word of ours.

Though nothing will have changed
when we turn away from the river
to the sacrament of sleep.

Earth Station

(Goonhilly Downs)

Tumuli, not hills. Cold
earthheaps with men and women in them,
femurs, teeth, four thousand years old,
easy to consider.

Unlike this briar with its punishing straps
drawing stripes on my reddening wrists now.
Unlike your bootlength, hesitant steps
into unstitched heather.

The wind will not be revealed as wind
until it's story. We say it was
'so strong we had to lean on it to stand'.
But really weather

is now. And it's now we can't know.
We can't hold what we feel,
only say that we felt. And so
learn to suffer.

Two silent huge bells turn away
from this trouble, are trained by our needs
not to feel, not to see.
Their commitment to other

places easy to believe in—
earthhopes with men and women in them
(Philadelphia, California) . . . 0101 . . .

Purr goes the receiver.

Purr purr. Purr purr.

Goonhilly Downs: The site of the satellite station in Cornwall which relays
telephone calls abroad. Also an iron age burial ground.

The Garden

She feels it like a shoulder of hair,
the garden, shrugging off the steamed, squeezed
eye of her kitchen window. Self-engendered chaos,
milky convolvulus, huge comet daisies. Tear
open the stocking of the leek pod and it frees
mathematically its globe, its light radiants.

But still she feels it hateful, August in its sweat,
the children filthy and barefoot ... angry woman
in a stained striped apron, sipping juice off a knife—
thick syrups of pounded rose hip and pulped fruit.
In bright air, between briar roses and a viney drain,
Arenea diadema sips the silk-spindled fly.

Her pet cat's a killer, a fur muff
curled fatly now in a catnest of hot
grass and goutweed. Of this morning's robin
too much was left—feathers, fluff,
feet, beak, the gorgeous throat caught
in the gored, delicate, perfectly balanced skeleton.

Whose Goat?

Broken bleats
from a half-built house
by the reefy unfeeling river
prefigure goat.

Where? Whose goat?

Who'd wall a goat up in cinderblocks?
A kind of goat closet full of hairy,
shadowy, strawy, obstinate
hopelessness of goat.

Only kid, really, but mammy and
all other times undone,
unhappened for her
in the huge push to get out.

121

So I grieve for her and her
sore forked head
rattling wire mesh like machinery,
for the pale hurt muzzle
pleading between pearl hooves.

It's beech I poke into the helpless
loop of her mouth. She meets
my labrador nostril to nostril, but
they breathe different languages.

I look my own language deep into the well
beneath the letter-box-black slit
in the gold mandala of her eye.
It finds a goat's ghost there,
lonely as snow. She's not
my goat, she's not my goat.

Somebody's collar of hospitality
is called 'I love that goat.'

Somebody's notion of living in the country
is building their own house slowly,
slowly around their own goat.

Giving Rabbit to my Cat Bonnie

Pretty Bonnie, you are quick as a rabbit,
though your tail's longer,
emphasizing suppressed disapproval,
and your ears are shorter—two
radar detectors set on swivels
either side of your skull, and your yawn
is a view of distant white spires—not
the graveyard jaw of this poor dead naked pink

rabbit, who like you, was a
technological success, inheriting a snazzy
fur coat, pepper-and-salt coloured, cosy,
and beautiful fur shoes with spiked toes.
You're both of you
better dressed than I am for most occasions.

Take off your shoes and suits, though,
what have you got?

Look puss, I've brought us a rabbit for supper.
I bought it in a shop.
The butcher was haggis-shaped, ham-coloured,
not a bit like you. His ears
were two fungi on the slab of his head.
He had a fat, flat face.
But he took your brother rabbit off a hook
and spread him on the counter like a rug,

and slice, slice, scarcely looking,
pulled the lovely skin off like a bag.
So, Bonnie, all I've brought us is food
in this silly pink shape—more like me, really.
I'll make a wine sauce with mushrooms, but will
you want this precious broken heart? this perfect liver?
See, protected in these back pockets, jewels?
Bonnie. What are you eating? Dear Bonnie, consider!

The Fish are all Sick

The fish are all sick, the great whales dead,
the villages stranded in stone on the coast,
ornamental, like pearls on the fringe of a coat.
Sea men, who knew what the ocean did,
turned their low houses away from the surf.
But new men, who come to be rural and safe,
add big glass views and begonia beds.

Water keeps to itself.
White lip after lip
curls to a close on the littered beach.
Something is sicker and blacker than fish.
And closing its grip, and closing its grip.

Sonnets for Five Seasons

For my father

This House

which represents you as my bones do, waits
all pores open, for the stun of snow. Which will come
as it always does, between breaths, between nights
of no wind and days of the nulled sun.
And has to be welcome. All instinct wants to anticipate
faceless fields, a white road drawn
through dependent firs, the soldered glare of lakes.

Is it wanting you here to want the winter in?
I breathe you back into your square house and begin
to live here roundly. This year will be between,
not in, four seasons. Do you hear already the wet
rumble of thaw? Stones. Sky. Streams.
Sun. Those might be swallows at the edge of sight
returning to last year's nest in the crook of the porchlight.

Complaint

'Dear God', they write, 'that was a selfish winter
to lean so long, unfairly, on the spring.
And now—this too much greed of seedy summer.
Mouths of the flowers unstick themselves and sting
the bees with irresistible dust. Iris
allow undignified inspection. Plain waste
weeds dress up in Queen Anne's lace; our mist
blue sky clouds heavily with clematis—

'Too much', they cry, 'too much. Begin again.'
The Lord, himself a casualty of weather,
falls to earth in large hot drops of rain.
The dry loam rouses in his scent, and under
him—moist, sweet, discriminate—the spring.
Thunder. Lightning. He can do anything.

Between

The wet and weight of this half-born English winter
is not the weather of those fragmentary half-true willows
that break in the glass of the canal behind our rudder
as water arrives in our wake—a travelling arrow
of now, of now, of now. Leaves of the water
furl back from our prow, and as the pinnate narrow
seam of where we are drives through the mirror
of where we have to be, alder and willow
double crookedly, reverse, assume a power
to bud out tentatively in gold and yellow, so
it looks as if what should be end of summer—
seeds, dead nettles, berries, naked boughs—
is really the anxious clouding of first spring.
... 'Real' is what water is imagining.

Stasis

Before the leaves change, light transforms these lucid
speaking trees. The heavy drench of August
alters, thins; its rich and sappy blood
relaxes where a thirst ago no rest
released the roots' wet greed or stemmed their mad
need to be more. September is the wisest
time—neither the unbearable burning word
nor the form of it, cooped in its cold ghost.

How are they sombre—that unpicked apple, red,
undisturbed by its fall; calm of those wasp-bored amethyst
plums on the polished table? Body and head
easy in amity, a beam between that must,
unbalanced, quicken or kill, make new or dead
whatever these voices are that hate the dust.

The Circle

It is imagination's white face remembers
snow, its shape, a fluted shell on shoot
or flower, its weight, the permanence of winter
pitched against the sun's absolute root.

All March is shambles, shards. Yet no amber
chestnut, Indian, burnished by its tent
cuts to a cleaner centre or keeps a summer
safer in its sleep. Ghost, be content.

You died in March when white air hurt the maples.
Birches knelt under ice. Roads forgot
their way in aisles of frost. There were no petals.

Face, white face, you are snow in the green hills.
High stones complete your circle where trees start.
Granite and ice are colours of the heart.

Transparencies

A Letter to my Sons

Your time with me ends with August, and now
August is over. Between Oxford and Cambridge—
that English triangle they make with London—
fields must be yellow harvested, as here in Wales.
Little straw-built cities, movable dolmens.
They look solid enough to believe in, stacked in bales.
 I carry my wound back upright in the car
 as if its grief could spill.

But it's a gift, too, this grief-grail, freedom to
love you without you. 'My sons' creates you abstract as
gold fields the windows slide behind your faces,
crossing by bus to grandparents whose good sense
still can't splinter to forgiveness, who'll find you,
like your music, alien as energy. And all they have.
 Later you'll look past me and your cleft childhood
 to their calm, whole house

where habit and reason—harvest of half a century's
lesson in upheaval—look solid enough to believe in,
if, by then, abstractions like 'the past' and 'mother'
make you cry—and like to cry. The act of memory's
a film we learn to make and watch so lives
can be performances. Worse than T.V.—
 to leave your tea mugs and *The Moon of Gomrath*
 plangent on a table

and, as if you were here, set off with the dog
to the riverpath, where yesterday the sun
struck slantwise, shafted, just as now. I see how
last year's leaves are almost this year's dust.
Papery thorn shapes ... maple ... alder ... stir
in a gust of passing. Molecular squall of gnats
        where the path's still hot. Leaves like syllables
        of light in a text of shadows.

This is a letter I'd never write if I could
send you counsel. Cicero, Polonius—thistles
preaching their beards to their blown seed. Oh,
it's your particular selves I need to hold
to the light as you cross the impossible lens of now
and now. Solid enough to believe ... until
        the river ripples under your melting faces
        mouthing at me from its thin windows.

THE FICTION-MAKERS

The Fiction-Makers

We were the wrecked elect,
the ruined few. Youth,
youth, the Café Iruña
and the bullfight set,
looped on Lepanto brandy
but talking 'truth'—
Hem, the 4 a.m. wisecrack,
the hard way in,
that story we were all at the end of
and couldn't begin—
we thought we were living now,
but we were living then.

Sanctified Pound, a knot
of nerves in his fist,
squeezing the Goddamn iamb
out of our verse,
making it new in his
archaeological plot—
to maintain 'the sublime'
in the factive? Couldn't be done.
Something went wrong
with 'new' in the Pisan pen.
He thought he was making now,
but he was making then.

Virginia, Vanessa,
a teapot, a Fitzroy fuss,
'Semen?' asks Lytton,
eyeing a smudge on a dress.
How to educate England
and keep a correct address
on the path to the river through
Auschwitz? Belsen?
Auden and Isherwood
stalking glad boys in Berlin—

they thought they were suffering now,
but they were suffering then.

Out of pink-cheeked Cwmdonkin,
Dylan with his Soho grin.
Planted in the fiercest of flames,
gold ash on a stem.
When Henry jumped out of his joke,
Mr Bones sat in.
Even you, with your breakable heart
in your ruined skin,
those poems all written
that have to be you, dear friend,
you guessed you were dying now,
but you were dying then.

Here is a table with glasses,
ribbed cages tipped back,
or turned on a hinge to each other
to talk, to talk,
mouths that are drinking or smiling
or quoting some book,
or laughing out laughter as candletongues
lick at the dark—
so bright in this fiction
forever becoming its end,
we think we are laughing now,
but we are laughing then.

Re-reading Jane

The memorial to Jane Austen in Winchester Cathedral reads:

In memory of JANE AUSTEN, youngest daughter of the late Rev^d
George Austen, formerly rector of Steventon in this county. She departed
this life on the 18th July, 1817, after a long illness supported with the
patience and the hopes of a Christian. The benevolence of her heart, the
sweetness of her temper, and the extraordinary endowments of her mind
obtained the regard of all who knew her and the warmest love of her
intimate connections. Their grief is in proportion to their affection. They
know their loss to be irreparable, but in their deepest affliction they are
consoled by a firm though humble hope that her charity, devotion, faith

and purity have rendered her soul acceptable in the sight of her
REDEEMER.

To women in contemporary voice and dislocation
she is closely invisible, almost an annoyance.
Why do we turn to her sampler squares for solace?
Nothing she saw was free of snobbery or class.
Yet the needlework of those needle eyes . . .
We are pricked to tears by the justice of her violence:
Emma on Box Hill, rude to poor Miss Bates,
by Mr Knightley's *were she your equal in situation—*
but consider how far this is from being the case
shamed into compassion, and in shame, a grace.

Or wicked Wickham and selfish pretty Willoughby,
their vice, pure avarice which, displacing love,
defiled the honour marriages should be made of.
She punished them with very silly wives.
Novels of manners? Hymeneal theology!
Six little circles of hell, with attendant humours.
For what do we live but to make sport for our neighbours
And laugh at them in our turn? The philosophy
paused at the door of Mr Bennet's century;
The Garden of Eden's still there in the grounds of Pemberley.

The amazing epitaph's 'benevolence of heart'
precedes 'the extraordinary endowments of her mind'
and would have pleased her, who was not unkind.
Dear votary of order, sense, clear art
and irresistible fun, please pitch our lives
outside self-pity we have wrapped them in,
and show us how absurd we'd look to you.
You knew the mischief poetry could do.
Yet when Anne Elliot spoke of *its misfortune*
to be seldom safely enjoyed by those who
enjoyed it completely, she spoke for you.

Waving to Elizabeth

For Elizabeth Bishop

For mapmakers' reasons, the transcontinental air routes
must have been diverted today, and Sunderland's stratosphere
is being webbed over by shiny almost invisible spider jets

creeping with deliberate intention across the skin like air,
each suspended from the chalky silk of its passing. Thready at
    first,
as if written by two, or four, fine felt nibs, the lines become
    cloudy
as the planes cease to need them. In freedom they dissolve. Just
as close observation dissipates in the wind of theory.

Eight or nine of them now, and all writing at once,
rising from the south on slow rails, slow arcs, an armillary
prevented by necessity from completing its evidence,
but unravelling instead in soft powdery stripes, which seem to be
the only clouds there are between what's simply here as park,
house, roof, road, car, etc. and the wide long view
they must have of us there, if they bother to look.
They have taken so much of us up with them, too—

money and newspapers, meals, toilets, old films, hot coffee—
yet the miles between us, though measurable, seem unreal.
I have to think, 'Here it is, June 19th, 1983.
I'm waving from a waste patch by the Thornhill School.'
As perhaps you think back from your trip through the cosmos,
'Here where I love it is no time at all. The geography
looks wonderful. This high smooth sea's more quiet than the
    map is,
though the map, relieved of mapmakers, looks imprisoned and
    free.'

The Blue Pool

After the painting by Augustus John

It is high summer by the blue pool.
Our heroine has left the safe house of her book
to repose on one arm in the shape of a girl
in this hungry man's painting of a blue pool
with a creamy shelf of dry mountains around it
and a tawny bronze tint to the white reflections.
This could be a hot day near a flooded quarry.
The flowing green dress, the moth-starred jerkin,
the dark bobbed hair are all parts of a story,
but its title and substance have no importance.

131

What *is* important is the book's colour, which is yellow.
In a child's picture the sun would be this colour,
and the view would fall away from the sun
like a symmetrical tent from a pole.
But in this adult landscape the sun's understood,
it's the undefined source of the light,
so the girl and her book have a moony existence—
as the mind indeed has when it ceases to see *as*
but returns pure reflections from the blue or brown
pools of its seeing. The girl could not possibly be reading.

She herself is the quick of the paint's observation
which allows her so sweetly to float out away from herself,
where for once she is perfectly happy, perfectly whole,
though she still keeps a finger on her place in the book.
The enamelled bright pages must have something in them,
in a minute she's sure to remember . . .
She is young, too, and wishes the painter were with her.
Soon she'll slip round the blank fearful page of his easel
to look at herself. Will the painting be like her?
She will think, she thinks, of something intelligent to say.

Where the Animals Go

The Beasts in Eden
cradle the returning souls of earth's animals.

The horse, limp cargo, craned down to the terrible quay,
is butchered into the heaven of his own hoofed kind.

The retriever mangled on the motorway, the shot
Alsatian by the sheepfold, the mutilated black-faced sheep—
they rise like steam, like cumulus, crowding in together,
each into the haunches of its archetype.

The drowned vole, the pheasant brought down with his fires,
the kitten in the jacket of its panicking fleas,
flying souls, furred, feathered, scaled, shelled, streaming
upward, upward through the wide thoughtless rose empyrean.

God absorbs them neatly in his green teeming cells.

There, sexed as here, they're without hurt or fear.
Heaven is honeycombed with their arrivals and entries.
Two of each Butterfly. Two of each Beetle.
A great Cowness sways on her full uddered way.
All kinds of Cat watch over the hive like churches.
Their pricked ears, pinnacles. Their gold eyes, windows.

Ailanthus with Ghosts

Their veins were white
but they still hung on with weak hands.
Their wings were dry,
but they still waved back at the wind,
'Just one more day. Just one more day.'

Then, very quietly, Monday night,
a frost-gun shot them away.
Imagine the whole population of Heaven
(Heaven was the name of the tree)
falling down simultaneously,

dazzling the root in its bed.
'What a beautiful star,' Heaven said.
Or might have if heavens could notice
the difference it makes to an earth
to be thatched with ghosts.

Shale

that comes to pieces in your hand
like stale biscuit; birth book
how many million years
left out in the rain. Break back

the pages, the flaking pages,
to reveal our own hairline habitations,
the airless museum in which we're
still chained into that still ocean,

while all this burly and stirring water—
motion in monotonous repetition—
washes with silt our Jurassic numbness,
the shelves of ourselves to which we will not return.

Bedded in shale, in its negative evidence,
this Venus shell is small as maybe she was.
The fan-shaped tracery of vertical ridges
could be fine-spread, radiant hair,

or proof of what we take to be
her temper—hot sluttishness loosened
by accident into cold mudslide,
preserving a hated symmetry, a hated elegance.

There is so little sheltered, kept, little
and frail, broken in excavation, half
buried, half broken, poor real child in the boulder
that finds the right shape of its mind

only at the moment of disintegration.
And yet—this clear cuneiform in rock;
this sea urchin humping its flower under
'low flying phantoms' . . . this flowing anemone.

Gannets Diving

The sea is dark
by virtue of its white lips;
the gannets, white,
by virtue of their dark wings.

Gannet into sea.

Cross the white bolt
with the dark bride.

Act of your name, Lord,
though it does not appear so
to you in the speared fish.

134

Making Poetry

'You have to inhabit poetry
if you want to make it.'

And what's 'to inhabit'?

To be in the habit of, to wear
words, sitting in the plainest light,
in the silk of morning, in the shoe of night;
a feeling, bare and frondish in surprising air;
familiar . . . rare.

And what's 'to make'?

To be and to become words' passing
weather; to serve a girl on terrible
terms, embark on voyages over voices,
evade the ego-hill, the misery-well,
the siren hiss of *publish, success, publish,
success, success, success.*

And why inhabit, make, inherit poetry?

Oh, it's the shared comedy of the worst
blessed; the sound leading the hand;
a wordlife running from mind to mind
through the washed rooms of the simple senses;
one of those haunted, undefendable, unpoetic
crosses we have to find.

Epitaph for a Good Mouser

Take, Lord, this soul of furred unblemished worth,
The sum of all I loved and caught on earth.
Quick was my holy purpose and my cause.
I die into the mercy of thy claws.

Hands

Made up in death as never in life,
mother's face was a mask
set in museum satin.

But her hands. In her hands,
resting not crossing on her paisley dress
(deep combs of her pores,

her windfall palms, familiar routes
on maps not entirely hers
in those stifling flowers), lay

a great many shards of lost hours
with her growing children. As when,
tossing my bike

on the greypainted backyard stairs,
I pitched myself up, through the screen door
arguing with my sister, 'Me? Marry?

Never! Unless I can marry a genius.'
I was in love with Mr Wullover,
a pianist.

Mother's hands moved *staccato* on a fat ham
she was pricking with cloves.
'You'll be lucky, I'd say, to marry a kind man.'

I was aghast.
If you couldn't *be* a genius, at least
you could marry one. How else would you last?

My sister was conspiring to marry her violin teacher.
Why shouldn't I marry a piano
in Mr Wullover?

As it turned out, Mr Wullover died
ten years before my mother.
Suicide on the eve of his wedding, O, to another.

No one said much about why at home. At school
Jenny told me in her Frankenstein whisper,
'He was gay!'

Gay? And wasn't it a good loving thing
to be gay? As good as to be kind
I thought then,

and said as much to my silent mother
as she wrung out a cloth until her knuckles shone,
white bone under raw thin skin.

On Watching a Cold Woman
Wade into a Cold Sea

The way that wintry woman
walked into the sea
was as if, in adultery,
she strode to her leman.

Something in the way she
shrugged off her daughters'
moping by the sea's hem
as if they were human

but she of the pedigree
and breed of Poseidon,
slicing through the breakers
with her gold-plated knees,
twisting up her hair
with a Medusan gesture,

something in the augury
she shook from her nature
made women look at women
over stiff cups of tea,
and husbands in their season
sigh suburbanly to see her.

Oh go dally with your children
or your dogs, naked sirs;
the venom of the ocean
is as kindness to hers.

137

In the Tunnel of Summers

Moving from day into day
I don't know how,
eating these plums now
this morning for breakfast
tasting of childhood's
mouth-pucker tartness,
watching the broad light
seed in the fences,
honey of barley,
gold ocean, grasses,
as the tunnel of summers,
of nothing but summers,
opens again
in my travelling senses.

I am eight and eighteen and eighty
All the Augusts of my day.

Why should I be, I be
more than another?
brown foot in sandal,
burnt palm on flaked clay,
flesh under waterfall
baubled in strong spray,
blood on the stubble
of fly-sweet hay—
why not my mother's, my
grandmother's ankle
hurting as harvest hurts
thistle and animal?
a needle of burning,
why this way or that way?

They are already building the long straw cemetery
where my granddaughter's daughter has been born
    and buried.

Willow Song

For Frances Horowitz

I went down to the railway
But the railway wasn't there.
A long scar lay across the waste
Bound up with vetch and maidenhair
And birdsfoot trefoils everywhere.
But the clover and the sweet hay,
The cranesbill and the yarrow
Were as nothing to the rose bay
    the rose bay, the rose bay,
As nothing to the rose bay willow.

I went down to the river
But the river wasn't there.
A hill of slag lay in its course
With pennycress and cocklebur
And thistles bristling with fur.
But ragweed, dock and bitter may
And hawkbit in the hollow
Were as nothing to the rose bay,
    the rose bay, the rose bay
As nothing to the rose bay willow.

I went down to find my love,
My sweet love wasn't there.
A shadow stole into her place
And spoiled the loosestrife of her hair
And counselled me to pick despair.
Old elder and young honesty
Turned ashen, but their sorrow
Was as nothing to the rose bay
    the rose bay, the rose bay,
As nothing to the rose bay willow.

O I remember summer
When the hemlock was in leaf.
The sudden poppies by the path
Were little pools of crimson grief,
Sick henbane cowered like a thief.

139

But self-heal sprang up in her way,
And mignonette's light yellow,
To flourish with the rose bay,
   the rose bay, the rose bay,
To flourish with the rose bay willow.

Its flames took all the wasteland
And all the river's silt,
But as my dear grew thin and grey
They turned as white as salt or milk.
Great purples withered out of guilt,
And bright weeds blew away
In cloudy wreathes of summer snow,
And the first one was the rose bay,
   the rose bay, the rose bay,
The first one was the rose bay willow.

Dreaming of the Dead

For Anne Pennington

I believe, but what is belief?

I receive the forbidden dead.
They appear in the mirrors of asleep
To accuse or be comforted.

All the selves of myself they keep,
From a bodiless time arrive,
Retaining in face and shape

Shifting lineaments of alive.
So whatever it is you are,
Dear Anne, bent smilingly grave

Over wine glasses filled by your fire,
Is the whole of your life you gave
To our fictions of what you were.

Not a shadow of you can save
These logs that crackle with light,
Or this smoky image I have—

Your face at the foot of a flight
Of wrought-iron circular stairs.
I am climbing alone in the night

Among stabbing, unmerciful flares.
Oh, I am what I see and know,
But no other solid thing's there

Except for the terrible glow
Of your face and its quiet belief,
Light wood ash falling like snow

On my weaker grief.

Black Grate Poems

*For Paul Winstanley and the former inhabitants
of his house and our house*

November

All saints and all souls,
martyrdom of the good days.
Daylight is smoke out of the dark's bonfire.
An old sun huddles in unclean caves.
But here, anyway, is this step,
now another step.
In imaginary fields, a tractor
sputters with purposes.
As black coal in our black grate
ignites in uncertain tongues,
birch-blaze thins over clinker
where the coke works were.

Household Gods

The room is silent except for the two hearth spirits.

The fire speaks out of the grate like a kindly tongue.
The man speaks out of the square screen like a god.

The fire burns slowly, holding itself back from burning.
The man speaks quickly, hurtling himself into particles.

Hold up your hands to the fire, and they, too, are fires.
Hold your hands up to the screen, and feel the premises of
    illusion.

Wherever you move, the fire pulls you close like a magnet.
Wherever you look, the screen intercepts your escape.

When the fire is worshipped, the resident cats will pray with
    you.
When the screen presides, it lashes the dog with its scream.

The fire has nothing to tell you; it waits for your thoughts.
The screen has to tell you everything except what you are.

In heaven, they will give you to fire to be consumed into
    freedom.
In hell, they will play you over and over on the tape of your
    dead life.

In hell, nothing you have done will be not watched.

Demolition

They have blown up the old brick bridge
connecting the coal works with the coke works.
Useful and unimposing,
it was ever a chapel of small waters,
a graceful arch toothworked with
yellow bricks notched into red bricks,
reflecting there sudden bright winks
from the Browney—an oval asymmetrical image
which must have delighted, as fisher-children,
these shiftless but solid grey men
who follow so closely the toil of its demolition.

The digger's head drops, grates, swings up,
yellow fangs slavering rubble and purple brickdust;
but the watchers wear the same grave, equivocal expression.
They might be grieving
(their fathers built it, or their fathers' fathers)
or they might be meaning
Boys won't be going to the mine no more.
Best do away with what's not needed.
That's Jock Munsey's lad in the cab there, surely.
Good job it's at home, not away on the telly.

February: Track to Lanchester

The Black Burn rattles into the brown Browney,
but the dominant colour of the season is silver,

bright tin of bare beechwood in light
diffused white out of one shallow cloud,

pewter at the heavier snow-black horizon where
intense hills—studded here, there, with live pylons—

ignite nearer railings, wires, roofs, windy larches,

between which, faint-breathing, much warmer mud
persuades rosy rags out of vertical birches.

Confusion of voices. Dispersal of finches.

The track, insubstantial as stone over mercury,
does really hold us, means to support us.

As it does those on motorbikes behind and before us
whose brown sputter throws up black grit in their faces.

A Prayer to Live with Real People

Let me not live, ever, without fat people,
the marshmallow flesh set thick on the muscular bone,
the silk white perms of sweet sixteen-stone ladies,
luscious as pom-poms or full blown perfumed magnolias,
with breasts like cottage loaves dropped into lace-knit sweaters,
all cream-bun arms and bottoms in sticky leathers.
O Russian dolls, O range of hills
rosy behind the glo-green park of the pool table,
thorns are not neater or sharper than your delicate shoes.

Let me not live, ever, without pub people,
the tattooed forearm steering the cue like a pencil,
the twelve-pint belly who adds up the scores in his head,
the wiry owner of whippets, the keeper of ferrets,
thin wives who suffer, who are silent, who talk with their eyes,
the girl who's discovered that sex is for she who tries.
O zebra blouse, O vampish back
blown like a lily from the swaying stalk of your skirt,
roses are not more ruthless than your silver-pink lipstick.

Let me live always and forever among neighbours like these
who order their year by the dates of the leek competitions,
who care sacrificially for Jack Russell terriers and pigeons,
who read very carefully captions in *The Advertiser* and *Echo*
which record their successes and successes of teams they
   support,
whose daughters grow up and marry friends' boys from Crook.
O wedding gifts, O porcelain flowers
twined on their vases under the lacelip curtains,
save me from Habitat and snobbery and too damn much literary
   ambition!

WINTER TIME

———◆◆◆◆———

Jarrow
For fr. Aelred

Talis ... vita hominum praesens in terris, ad conparationem eius, quod
nobis incertum est, temporis, quale cum te residente ad caenam cum
ducibus ac ministris tuis tempore brumali ... adveniens unus passerum
domum citissime pervolaverit; qui cum per unum ostium ingrediens, mox
per aliud exierit ... Mox de hieme in hiemem regrediens, tuis oculis
elabitur.

Bede, *Historia Ecclesiastica Gentis Anglorum*

Would want to paint them,
those town bright boys
at the dead end of the track
where it coils down away
from church and mound
leaving almost an island
as it once must have been
when Bede set his *Lucem Vitae*
lightly on the pages of
these empty mudflats.

One thousand three hundred years
to set that orange apparatus
(for loading coal?) cleanly
in the mouth of the Tyne
and decide to abandon it,
there, beneath that regiment
of scarred blue oil drums.
The scene looks set for
a study of bad times
in the lap of old times,

dead machinery teasing the live
hooting youths who have
nothing to do here in their
circus clothes, their peaked pink
hair like traffic cones ...

The more civilized the civilized,
the more barbarian the barbarians.
Such vivid colours, though,
like shipworks, in what
seems to be one more picture of

enough. A passing sparrow would
see it, crossing from winter
into winter—the cracked black
skin of the tide between ripples of
couch grass, the blue sheet of river
rusty with ships, the cranes
against the monks' sky, crossed by high
pylons in their chains of power.
Lightbearers. *Lucifera.* Latin would have
named them, as the kneeling church

outlasts them in its green patch of
ruin. I would like to paint
a sparrow's view—the prefabs
(now the monks' cells), the heaps of
sweet timber by the sawmill's warehouse
fenced from an old blind horse
in a field; the polished brass lamps
along the walks, a smudge of kids
in the distance. I would, in my painting
be a brushstroke ... *Talis vita in terris* ...

Naming the Flowers

makes no difference to the flowers.
These inside-out parasols,
orb webs on crooked needles,
grey filmy cups in the clockwork
of summer goatsbeard

are to themselves not 'seeds',
not 'systems of distribution',
never the beards of goats,

but to us they anticipate
bare patches, old age, winter-time.

They tell us to pronounce now
all that we wish to keep.

My fields of recollection
already are yellow with toadflax.
Wheels of sky-blue chicory
purl into purple angelica;
hogweed is taller than my sons.

The path I will follow is
shocking with unfinished steeples;
'foxglove', I'll say, then 'balsam',
'rose bay willow herb', 'red campion'.

I'll note particularly
the pinched liquorice temper of my fingers,
pods of sweet cicely. Scabious
will be last into my grey-blue coma,
reminding me of heaven,
the shell-frail colour of harebells.

In winter-time my bare patch
will be heavy with names.
I am only a namer.
Only the names are seeds.

———◆••◆———

Acknowledgements

These poems have appeared in *Living in America* (Generation Press, The University of Michigan), 1965, *Reversals* (Wesleyan University Press), 1969, *Correspondences* (Wesleyan University Press, and Oxford University Press), 1974, *Travelling Behind Glass* (OUP), 1974, *Enough of Green* (OUP), 1977, *Minute by Glass Minute* (OUP), 1982, *The Fiction-Makers* (OUP), 1985, *Black Grate Poems* (Inky Parrot Press), 1985, and *Winter Time* (MidNag), 1986.